MW01608485

East of the Red:

Early Ukrainian Settlements 1896-1930 Vol. 1

Michael Ewanchuk

Copyright© 1998 by Michael Ewanchuk

All rights reserved. No part of this book may be reproduced in any form by any means, electronic or mechanical including photocopying and recording, without written permission from the author, except by a reviewer who may quote brief passages in a review to be printed in a magazine or newspaper.

Canadian Cataloguing in Publication Data

Ewanchuk, Michael, 1908-

East of the Red : early Ukrainian settlements, 1896-1930

Includes bibliographical references and index.
ISBN 0-9695779-3-1 (v. 1)

1. Ukrainians--Manitoba--History. 2. Immigrants--Manitoba--History. 3. Frontier and pioneer life--Manitoba. I. Title.

FC3400.U4 E828 1998 971.27'4 C98-920214-3
F1065.U4 E83 1998

Published November 1998

Michael Ewanchuk, Publisher, Winnipeg, Manitoba

Printed by Derksen Printers, Steinbach, Manitoba and Bound in Canada

Dedicated to

My, now departed, School Teacher
and
Friend

Mr. Peter Humeniuk

East of the Red: First Ukrainian Settlements
Volume I

Foreword

The Ukrainian diaspora in Canada had its origins in 1892 when a small group of settlers took homestead land in east-central Alberta. For the next three years with the exception of a few the Ukrainians who came to Canada followed this first group and settled alongside their compatriots in Alberta, laying the foundations of what could eventually become the largest Ukrainian settlement in the West. It was not until 1896 that the first Ukrainians arrived in Manitoba to claim their homesteads in the bush country east of the Red River.

The story of this migration from what were then the Austrian Crown Lands of Halychyna and Bukovyna to Manitoba is both complex and fascinating. History is sometimes shaped by the actions of determined individuals, and sometimes by happenstance. We can see all of this at work in the story of the Stuartburn settlement of southeastern Manitoba. Without the determined efforts of Dr. Osyp Oleskiw to persuade Ukrainians to emigrate to Canada rather than Brazil, Manitoba would be a very different place, and the poorer for it. As Michael Ewanchuk recounts in *East of the Red*, it was Oleskiw who organized and sent over the first party of emigrants who settled in Manitoba, choosing land near to the site of present-day Gardenton. This party of immigrants was the first, certainly one of the first, to include emigrants from Bukovyna, and was led by Kyrylo Genik, who later played a significant role in the settlement process through his many years working as an interpreter and colonization agent for the Department of the Interior.

The immigrants brought little with them in terms of material possessions, only the clothes on their backs and the few essentials that could be packed into a trunk and hauled thousands of miles to the New World. Nevertheless, they brought with them an ancient and rich culture, with a distinctive language, folklore, religion, and building traditions. Within a few years, even while they were still hacking homesteads out of the bush, they began to mark their presence in the landscape, building houses and churches in the distinctive Ukrainian style, and shortly thereafter organizing reading groups, National Homes and school districts. Their path was seldom smooth, for the land in southeastern Manitoba was of marginal quality, best suited, as they would later ironically remark, for raising crops of stones! Hard work and dogged determination enabled them to survive on their bush homesteads, to overcome the prejudice against them, to educate their children and give them the opportunity to fulfil their potential in Canadian society. What they achieved is truly remarkable. *East of the Red* recounts all of this and more.

Michael Ewanchuk has written extensively on the subjects of Ukrainian settlement and pioneer life and is well qualified to do so. His father was a pioneer of the Gimli district and he spent his early life immersed in a pioneer milieu. After receiving his education in Gimli and at the University of Manitoba, in 1930 he taught briefly at Svoboda School near Stuartburn, before his career took him further afield. Now retired after a distinguished career as an educator he has devoted his time to recording and writing the history of the people and the places he knows so well. His contributions have been recognized by the Shevchenko Society, which awarded him the Shevchenko Medal for his contributions to Ukrainian life and by the University of Winnipeg and the University of Manitoba which have both awarded him the honorary degree of Doctor of Laws.

John C. Lehr
Department of Geography
University of Winnipeg

Introduction

As a rule any book dealing with historical development of a country is many years in preparation, and the information for its content is gleaned from many sources and from many people. So it has been in the case of this volume: it goes back to the early thirties.

During the early thirties, the horrendous depression was setting in and times were getting more difficult. The period of the financial setback for the farmers was taking root. Such conditions make people recall the difficult times their parents and they had lived through; the times when they first settled on the homesteads some twenty/thirty miles east of Dominion City. They were also recalling the year 1896; they were recalling the eminent Dr. Joseph Oleskiw who induced the land-hungry Ukrainian peasant-farmers to leave their native land where the soil was fertile and the climate was Mediterranean and to emigrate to Western Canada.

It was during the early thirties that the author of this volume was engaged as a teacher in one of the schools east of Stuartburn where the settlement had its base. It was located on a trail some called "narodna doroha" that ran from Stuartburn to the Shevchenko area. The name of the school was Svoboda, meaning "Freedom". It so happened that the school was located right in the centre of a semi-circle with a twelve mile diameter; with the hamlets of Vita and Stuartburn at each end of it. At the end of the radius going directly south was Gardenton. It was within the bounds of this semi-circle that the landowners were still the original Oleskiw settlers or their descendants, many of them coming to Canada in 1896 as children or teenagers.

The author lived in the teacherage beside the school and on weekends walked to the hamlets to shop, get his mail and to visit with other teachers. As a rule on Thursday during the winter season, four farmers of the district came to visit him. They were intelligent, progressive and sensible men, Wasyl Smook, Julian Cesmistruk, Yakiw Prociw and Iwan Lucyk. The conversations were of a serious nature and much was of a recall type about the early years of the settlement.

And then in the hamlets, in the evenings, local farmers met and in conversation recalled, and relived the pioneer days. In Stuartburn Mr. John Probizhansky, the storekeeper, was post master and was only sixteen when his father settled on a homestead. He lived through good days and some evil times. The attitude of the early Anglos and some of the Germans to the Ukrainians was abusive, and antagonistic and the Ukrainians were condemned in no uncertain terms.

In Gardenton there were local businessmen and in their stores local farmers met and discussed the difficulties of life in the swamplands. Here they lived closer to the American border and many did get employment in Minnesota and North Dakota and shopped in the stores. To maintain Cana-

dian customers the attitudes of the Americans seemed more tolerant.
In Vita the discussions were more political in nature and Messers Bodnarchuk, Uhryniuk, Kulachkowski, Machula and Kolisnyk were all proud of the cultural development that took place after the local community centre was established. Here they were proud of the leading roles taken by the women and the fine women's organization that led the way to finer social life.

Many discussions were written down and kept for future reference. Many interviews were made in later years, and research was carried out in the Canadian Archives and also in the archives in Winnipeg. The background information was checked and verified and all put together to constitute the content of this volume.

As the reader proceeds reading this volume, it will soon become apparent that the first Ukrainian settlers in Manitoba embraced Canadianism from the start; for it ensured them "Life and Liberty"; however, in their pursuit of happiness – particularly during the first thirty years in the land - they had to wend a long and thorny trail.

Michael Ewanchuk
July 28, 1998

Acknowledgements

In the first place the author wishes to express his sincere thanks to men and women, some close friends, for agreeing to be interviewed and to have their interviews published. My thanks also go to the archival, personnel that was willing to assist in providing access to source material and original records and correspondence which helped with interpretation of materials for this book. And I cannot forget the encouragement received from my dear late wife, Muriel, for her assistance and encouragement to start on a two volume project to record the pioneer days of the Ukrainian settlers east of the Red River.

It would be unfair at this point not to thank my friends and associates of the Interlake and Gimli Ukrainian Historical Society: V. Rev. John, A. Melnyk, president; Deacon Michael Woroby, vice-president; Miss Anne Smigil; Mr. Bill Solpya and Dr. Tony Kuz, past president, for the interest shown in the project and the encouragement provided. My thanks also go to my friend, Prof. J. C. Lehr of the University of Winnipeg for his advice and discussion of the approach to the project.

Finally I am deeply indebted to the Canadian Ukrainian Foundation of Taras Schevchenko that so kindly provided financial assistance toward the publishing of East of the Red, else I would have had to assume the total cost of publication myself.

Dr. Michael Ewanchuk

Part I
Immigration to the Canadian West

Chapter I
Social and Political Conditions in Ukraine

In mid nineteenth century the Hapsburg Empire was in an advanced stage of disintegration. In Imperial Russia radicalism was on the march. The 1848 proclamation that serfdom was being abolished in Austria - Hungary added a new dimension to the aspirations of the long-suffering and exploited population of Central Europe: The peasants were no longer bound by the dictates of the lords of large manors. However, the vestige of freedom gained did not give the peasant a chance to acquire more land to be able to support his family. He, therefore, had his freedom limited by having to work for the lord of the manor. And if any land was available, the peasant lacked the requisite means to acquire it. There was yet another burden: the Hapsburgs required that all men on reaching maturity report for a three year period of military training. This the peasants found to be a continuation of exploitation of manhood. And children had to go to work to help them - opportunities for education were limited.

However, after completing the period of military training men did have an opportunity to seek employment - though seasonal - in other lands, mostly Prussia. Employment in other lands provided the average man with information about the New World where land and labour opportunities were available. This New World was the U.S.A. a democracy where all men were considered relatively free.

Consequently, toward the end of the nineteenth century, the populations in that part of Ukrainian territory, known as Halychyna, now popularly called Western Ukraine began to undergo a period of national re-awakening and a change in social attitudes intensified. Opposition to foreign overlordship and to political control grew.

In time, however, the Ukrainians began to show progress - to advance culturally and develop new pride in their traditions. A historical revival appeared, led by men who managed to get a higher education and go into professions and also by the more progressive clergy of the Ukrainian Catholic church. They began to organize enlightenment groups, "Prosvita" and to form circles where those capable of reading would read to the progressive yet illiterate peasants. Consequently, their horizons widened.

There were sections of the country before 1848 where the peasants agreed to pay taxes in lieu of being bound to the lord of the manor providing free labour three days a week. Such was the case in the Kolomyja region. In this region schools were established sooner and a gymnasium soon came into being, giving many younger people an opportunity to acquire a higher education, and go into professions.

A Chance to View Democracy

Across the Atlantic a young country, known as the United States of America, was progressing economically at a rapid pace. The eastern states were getting rapidly industrialized. The industrial centres needed energy to operate their factories. There was plenty of coal in Pennsylvania, but they needed miners. True there was an in flock of miners from Ireland, but more was needed and soon they began to attract miners from Central Europe, and the Slavs came: Chechs, Poles, Hungarians and along with them Ukrainians. The Ukrainians who left informed others of the opportunities in the New Land and by 1870 there appeared nuclei of Ukrainian community centres in the coal-mining areas. Before long missionaries came to minister to the emigrees, and foremost among them was Rev. Iwan Wolanski.*

Brazilian Agents

As Poles, Germans, Chechs were leaving for the U.S.A., the steamship magnates, mostly Germans, found that there were opportunities for the land - hungry Europeans to settle on land in Brazil. And soon they were transporting people across the Atlantic; Polish and German colonies were formed in southern Brazil. Then agents appeared in Central Europe to induce Ukrainians to settle in Brazil. The special inducement was that trans-Atlantic transportation would be provided free; the Brazilian Government would cover the costs. In 1892 many Ukrainians sailed for the Parana region via Italian ports.

Settlers for Canada: The Nebeliv Group

In 1891 Ukrainian families joined the Germans to settle in what is now Alberta and around Saltcoats, Saskatchewan. Two men, however, became trail blazers as far as Manitoba was concerned. The two were Wasyl Eleniak and Iwan Pillipiw. They arrived in Winnipeg and established contact with the Mennonite farmers of the Gretna area who spoke their language as they had lived for many years in the Ukraine. (When the Mennonites came to Manitoba in 1874, it seems that there were some Ukrainians among them.) After harvesting in the Gretna area Iwan Pillipiw returned to his village in the Ukraine to encourage other settlers to emigrate to Canada and to bring out his and Mr. Eleniak's family to Manitoba. Wasyl Eleniak, however, remained in Gretna.

For his efforts to encourage the Ukrainian farmers to emigrate, Iwan Pillipiw was arrested and imprisoned. However, twelve families arrived in Winnipeg and left for Alberta in 1892. Iwan Pillipiw finally came and also settled in

* He signed his name Wolanski, and in correspondence used John instead of Iwan. See Appendix 3.

Alberta. Wasyl Eleniak worked in Gretna area for five years and should be given credit for being the first Ukrainian to establish a home in Manitoba. In 1892 Wasyl Yatchew was the first to establish a home in Winnipeg.

Wasyl Yatchew also from the Nebeliv area came with his wife and did go to Gretna, but it is not known whether he established contact with Eleniak who was later joined by Wisnowich. Eleniak worked for the farmers herding cattle, but he actually was indentured for five years. It may, therefore, be that Mr. Yatchew did not stay in the Gretna area avoiding indenture. After a few years, the Yatchews left Winnipeg for Beausejour.

Fig. 1 Dr. Joseph Oleskiw

Brazilian Disappointments

Although the Ukrainian "colonists" received free transportation to Brazil, on arrival there, they found that the living costs and cost of equipment were high - there was no employment. Therefore, what they saved on transportation, they expended to get settled in the jungle regions of Parana. From the start misfortunes beset them: fever was decimating their young people, and the attacks of the natives made life unbearable. When news of the untenable conditions reached Ukraine and the Ukrainian miners in the U.S.A., Rev. Wolanski and his wife then established in Pennsylvania set out to investigate conditions in Brazil. Tragedy, however, beset them in Jio de Janairo: Mrs. Wolanski died of yellow fever. On return to the U.S.A. Rev. Wolanski reported his findings to the Ukrainian press to dissuade further settlement in South America.

In Lviv, Ukraine Rev. Wolanski's report on the plight of Ukrainian settlers in Brazil came to the attention of Prof. Joseph Oleskiw. Having heard about the German settlers and the Nebeliv group that went to Canada, he, a competent geographer, began to study literature about the new country and then established contact with Sir Charles Tupper the Canadian High Commissioner in London. He then made a trip to London and with the Commissioner's guidance and the offer from the C.P.R. to provide him with a free passage to Canada, he started to make preparations for a visit, at the same time making a press release suggesting that prospective emigrees withhold leaving for Brazil, until he had a chance to investigate conditions and opportunities in Canada.

The Ukrainian Lord Selkirk

Dr. Joseph Oleskiw may be called the Ukrainian Lord Selkirk. He was very much concerned that the agents of the Brazilian Government were responsible for many Ukrainian settlers leaving for the Brazilian jungle where they were meeting with unprecedented difficulties. He, therefore, decided to explore whether conditions for settlement were more favourable in Canada.

Dr. Oleskiw was a professor of agriculture in a gymnasium in the Ukraine and the right person to make a personal survey of the "New Land". On Thursday July 25, 1895 he left the city of Lviv accompanied by a well-to-do farmer, Iwan Dorundiak, and stopped in London where he had a conference with Sir Charles Tupper, the then Canadian High Commissioner. On Tuesday, August 12 they arrived in Canada, and after a conference with the officials of the Department of Immigration plans were made for his sea to sea trip.

Before returning to Europe he visited Rev. Nestor Dmytriw, a Ukrainian Catholic clergyman and editor of a Ukrainian newspaper, Svoboda, who was then living in Mount Carmel, Pennsylvania.

In 1895 during his first and only visit to Canada, Dr. Oleskiw had an opportunity to travel as far as the west coast and while in the Edmonton area he established as contact with a few Ukrainian settlers there. In the meantime Iwan Dorundiak appraised the situation in the Saltcoats area where there were a few Ukrainian settlers.

Dr. Oleskiw in Manitoba

The colonization agents took Dr. Oleskiw south to see the Mennonite settlements west of Emerson in the Gretna area. Being fluent in German he could discuss conditions of life with them. In the Red River Valley he was impressed with the rich black soil, and so much more impressed with the mode of cultivation: imagine a farmer seated on a gang plough and ploughing land that he did not have to clear by cutting down a tree or by picking up a stone. He had a vision, as Pierre Berton states, that in this fine country the land-hungry, politically-repressed Ukrainian farmers would do well. More importantly the opening of the gates to Canada would, at the same time, divert the emigration from going to Brazil.

It is difficult to determine which Ukrainians who were living in Canada Dr. Oleskiw and Mr. Dorundiak contacted. Dr. Oleskiw, however, received considerable information about their start in the Edmonton area.

There is no doubt that while in Manitoba he contacted both the Gretna people and Wasyl Yatchew in Winnipeg. It appears he was not only impressed with the richness of the land around Edmonton and south of Winnipeg, but also with the rapid advance his countrymen were making economically in the Edmonton region.

And as for Wasyl Yatchew, Pierre Berton writes:

> ....he came in 1892 with only $40.00, in 1895 he owned a house in Winnipeg, two cows and had a nest egg of $120.00
> Yurko Paish had even managed to send home $120.00 - a small fortune. Dmytro Wizynowich had also come with only $40.00 in 1893 and had been able to save $400.00[1]

It's no wonder that on his return to Ukraine he wrote a booklet.[2] This booklet was read by the peasants in the provinces of Halychyna and Bukovyna and many were hoping that they would soon be able to leave for Canada.

The booklets published were to a great degree responsible in developing interest among the Ukrainian peasants in emigrating to Canada. He also met with prominent Ukrainians including clergymen of the Ukrainian Catholic church and reported on his tour of Canada. The pamphlets were distributed by the Prosvita Society and became widely read by the land-hungry peasants.

"Dr. Oleskiw's booklets," writes Dr. Vladimir J. Kaye, "About Free Lands" and "About Emigration" published in 1895 were read by thousands of peasant farmers in village halls throughout the land. One of these booklets came to the newly established library of "Prosvita" reading hall in the village of Senkiw in the district of Zalishchyky...[3]

Zalishchyky is located close to the Dnister* River in the southwest corner of the rectangle. (See Fig. 2)

Dr. Oleskiw was a remarkable and a brilliant man: he was able to carry correspondence with the Canadian immigration officials using the "trilingual approach": he was thinking in Ukrainian, translating his thoughts in German and then with the aid of a German-English dictionary was able to communicate with the Canadian immigration authorities in English.

1 Pierre Berton: The Promised Land: Settling the West, 1896 - 1914. McClelland Stewart, Toronto, 1984, p.3
2 Also read. V. J. Kaye, Early Ukrainian Settlements in Canada 1895 - 1900. p. 29
3 V. J. Kaye, p.136
* Other spelling variations: "Dniester" or "Dneister".

Fig. 2 Map showing towns and villages around Senkiw in Western Ukraine.

Reactions to Dr. Oleskiw's Reports

The two of the Oleskiw's booklets and his meeting with the Ukrainian intelligencia created a keen interest in the Oleskiw's "Land of Promise" not only among the land-hungry peasants, but also among those who wanted to provide a better future for their children. And what added additional credence to the Oleskiw report was that his claims were substantiated by his companion Iwan Dorundiak. "The claims of a romantic intellectual", said the peasants, "are substantiated by a well-to-do farmer."

Consequently, as Dr. Oleskiw opened the flood gates to Canada, the tide of immigration to Brazil diminished considerably.

Chapter 2
Ukrainian Settlers Leave for Canada

In 1895 Dr. Oleskiw's booklet about free lands in Canada created a feverish interest among the peasants in the village of Senkiw on the Dnister River.

Village of Senkiw (Synkiw)

As recorded by Joseph Kohut[1] who was born there, the village was a very attractive place to live. The peasants in this village were well organized, they had beautiful churches and a community centre where a Prosvita library was located, and in this library the peasantry were able to read about the "Promised Land" where each could acquire 113 morgens[2] of free land for $10.00 With little land available for sale in Ukraine to establish young people as independent farmers, emigration to Canada spelled a better future.

After discussing the contents of Oleskiw's booklet, the villagers decided to send a delegation of two to meet with him in Lviv. The two members who went, and subsequently came to Canada, were Wasyl Stefura and Jacob Shelep

When the two returned they reported most positively about the opportunities and advantages of emigrating to Canada, stressing Oleskiw's recommendation that only peasants who were in sound financial circumstances should emigrate.

He also recommended to the settlers that it was advisable for them to take along their farming tools and portable implements. As for the tradesmen, weavers, potters, cabinet makers, tailors and blacksmiths, they should take their tools as they may have an opportunity to start some type of manufacturing.

On receiving the report, the Senkiw farmers began to make plans and preparations to leave. Some sold their property and a sizeable group was getting in readiness to leave. Joseph Kohut in his reminiscences mentions such names as Nykola Kohut, Onufry Smuk, Jacob Shelep, Iwan Salamandyk and Iwan Storozuk. And from across the Dnister River in the Province of Bukovyna from the village of Bridok, came the Wasyl Zahara family.

In getting the Senkiw group ready to leave for Canada to settle in Manitoba, Dr. Oleskiw included some families from Borschiw and several highlanders from Bereziw of the Kolomyja region. The Bereziw sample had among them a qualified school teacher, Cyril (Kyrilo) Genik. Mr. Genik could not get a position in state schools due to his radical views, and was engaged in agriculture. There could have not been a better man to lead the trail-blazers into the

---

1 Joseph Kohut, My Reminiscences, Rev. Stephen Semchuk, editor, 1958, p.1.

2 Joseph Oleskiw, About Free Lands pro vilnij zemli

province of Manitoba. He accepted the challenge and carried out his responsibilities exceptionally well. Come the end of June 1896, the Manitoba group left to be transported across the Atlantic. The busiest man in the group was Mr. Genik: using his German-English dictionary he was acquiring the rudiments of the English language.

However, the Genik-led group was not the first of the Oleskiw settlers to depart for Canada. Preceding this group was the first group that left in the spring of 1896 under the guidance of Joseph Oleskiw's brother, Wolodymyr. This group in arriving in Winnipeg in June 1896 was directed into the Whitemouth-Brokenhead area. However, on investigating conditions there rejected the region and left for Edmonton. They were a group of over one hundred souls with the heads of families and single men who after paying for their ocean-crossing carried a sum of $7,200 in cash.

Though the people who left Ukraine for the Canada where they saw a bright future for themselves and their children, the leaving their dear ones whom they would likely never see again was traumatic. Here we have the reminiscences of one who left Ukraine as a twelve-year-old boy.

Leaving the Ukraine

> My father sold his fields, his orchard and his home. He sold his cows, his horses and other things. Much was given to relatives. We were leaving for Canada. However, we waited to celebrate Easter in our native village.
>
> On Easter Sunday for the last time, I snag "Christ is Risen!" with the chaunters and when I got out of the church at the end of the service the boys and girls encircled me to bid me farewell. Already I looked different than they for my parents bought me clothing that the boys and girls wore in the large town of Kopychentsi. They all asked me to write to them from Canada, one little boy, Nykola, said, "Paul, when you train some of those wild horses of the Canadian steppes, you will be able to come and visit us at Christmas."

On Monday the wagons were loaded with trunks, crates, hand-trunks, wicker boxes and duffel bags and many women and children who had bid farewell to their dear ones sat waiting in the wagons many of them in tears. Then the parish priest, Rev. Barwinsky, drove past each wagon and sprinkled Holy Water on the emigrants. When he reached the lead wagon, he stopped and spoke briefly:

> My Dear Children, you are departing from your native hearths like birds from their nests. May God guide you and guard you from all evil. Learn to love your new country and your neighbors. I am bidding you farewell from your parish, your village and your kin. Do not leave your church and your traditions. Don't forget your native land. Maintain your language as you learn yet another. Don't forget about your parents, your brothers and sisters. We pray for your safety and happiness. May the Lord lead you!
>
> When he made the third sign of the cross and said, "Amen", his driver, fiacre,

guided the team in front and a large procession followed him. One man carried a cross and others carried banners. The lead wagon and the other wagons began to follow them. As we passed along the road leading out of the village the people stood at their gates and waved us their farewells. Soon we reached the end of the village and Reverend Barwinsky's buggy disappeared on the side road, the people who led the procession stopped and lowered the banners as each wagon passed.

We were out in the open fields and as I was walking beside the wagon that was taking us to the railway station, I turned around to look yet once more at our village: it never looked more beautiful to me. And I, a carefree twelve-year-old village lad, broke into heavy sobbing.

After a while my Mother called to me and asked me to climb up and ride. I sat beside her for a while and then leaning my head on her shoulder, I fell asleep.

It was dark when I was awakened by the hissing sound of the steam locomotive and heard one wagonner call out in a loud voice, "Peter, hold the horses!"

It was very dark when we left the Ternopil station and I came to sit beside my Mother. "You are hungry," she said. After satisfying my hunger with cold fried chicken, buttered paska* and an apple I fell asleep and left Ukraine forever.

The people reached the German part of Hamburg by train where they disembarked, and from there they took a "small boat" to Liverpool where they transferred to a large ship in which they crossed the Atlantic to reach Halifax. Then from Halifax they arrived in Winnipeg by train. This journey took them about three weeks.

Fig. 1 Micheal Stashyn the oldest living pioneer of 1896 on his 99th birthday in November 1987 with all 20 great-grand-children in Vancouver, B.C.

* paska, white Easter bread.

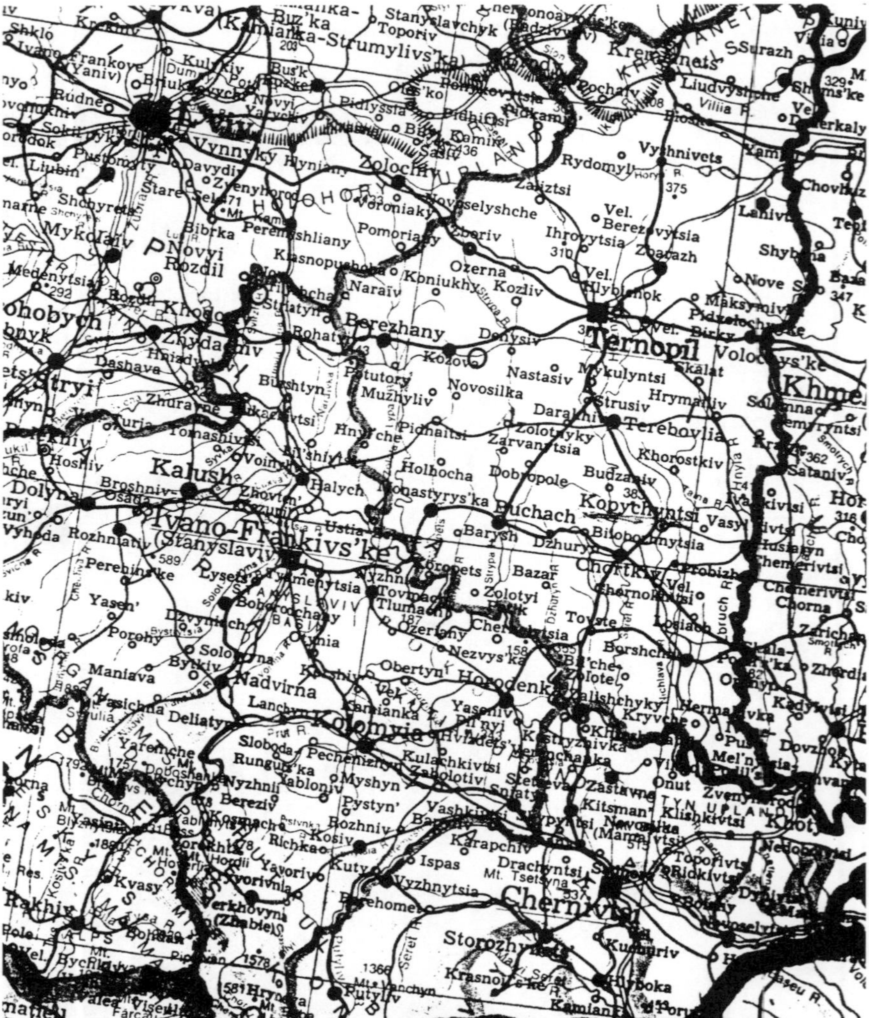

Fig. 2 Showing Ukrainian provinces of Halychyna and Bukovyna from which most of the settlers came.

Chapter 3

Oleskiw Settlers Arrive

A year after Dr. Oleskiw's tour of Canada and his visit to southern Manitoba, the first contingent of Ukrainian settlers bound for Manitoba arrived. They reached Winnipeg "...on the 25th of July...(1896) and were made comfortable at the Dominion Immigration Building."[1]

Under the guidance of Immigration officials, two delegations were formed: one to investigate opportunities for settlement in the Whitemouth-Brokenhead region (likely the area around the present Elma hamlet); the other to investigate conditions in the southern part of the Red River region, that is, east of the river.

On July 31, 1896, J. W. Wendelbo and the three Oleskiw delegates left for Steinbach (by a horse drawn democrat) to see:

> ...(how) their former neighbours prospered in the country.
>
> (at the end of the day)...the delegates were very much surprised and pleased with what they had seen...[2]

August 3...we followed the north-east side of the river until we reached Tp.2, Range 6E. where we found the land very satisfactory...[3]

August 1, this delegation with Cyril* Genik as leader left for Brokenhead and Whitemouth, but also returned rejecting settlement in the area.

> ...seemingly not satisfied with what they had seen of the country near Brokenhead and Whitemouth, but were desirous of obtaining free homesteads...[4]

There were disappointments, too. Dr. Oleskiw and immigration officials would have liked to have the first group settle in the Dauphin region, but the railway had not as yet reached that point by August 1896.

> On the other hand, the Steinbach delegates "having had time to describe the district we visited, (Wendelbo recorded) - 26 heads of families at once decided to form a settlement, and the colony was named Ruthenia."[5]

A small number, however, decided to settle on river lots in the St. Norbert area paying $11.00 an acre for the land.

According to Prof. J. C. Lehr, evidently Archbishop Langevin wanted the Ukrainians to settle in small holdings to form a village type of settlements.

---

1 Hugo Carstens to H. H. Smith, November 25/96 (370321) PA.
2 John W. Wendelbo to H. H. Smith, August 8, 1896 (410595) Winnipeg, MB.
3 Ibid
* Cyril or Kerylo
4 Ibid
5 Ibid

He selected St. Norbert and East Selkirk as suitable locations.

> - Tuesday August 11, 1896: It was decided that 24 or 26 families would proceed by train to Dominion City and from there by wagons to take possession of homesteads.[6] (The C.P.R. provided free transportation)

They were transported by wagon to a farmer's yard close to the Roseau River eighteen miles east of Dominion City and accommodated in Ramsey's barn where the women had a chance to do some washing while the men were away selecting homesteads.

Regrettably on reaching the Roseau River where the settlers were to cross to form the new colony, both the immigration officials and the Oleskiw settlers encountered the first problem: the survey posts demarcating townships and sections east of the Roseau River and north of Houle's store were difficult to locate. The officials, consequently, took the following action:

> Early the next morning, I was at work, and as there was no sign of lines, I began cutting new ones starting from a mound of the South West corner of the SW ¼ of Section 20 T.2 RGE.[7]

The immigration officials gave the settlers undivided attention and after the settlers made entries for their homesteads, they found that only the even numbered sections were made available to them thus separating them to a degree from each other: and it wasn't the best land either.

"The Township in which this colony is located appears to me to be somewhat low and as there is no drainage, the land settled upon will be flooded in spring."[8]

Ipso facto, by settling east of the Red River the Ukrainians had to accept decades of flooding.

Though the association with the settlers was brief – the officials formed a good opinion of them:

> The people seem to me on the whole as being frugal and industrious and would get along well in this country, if they only had more means to start farming.[9]

---

6 Ibid

7 August 25, 1896, J. Turenne, Clerk of Dominion Lands reported (PA 411031)

8 Ibid

9 Ibid

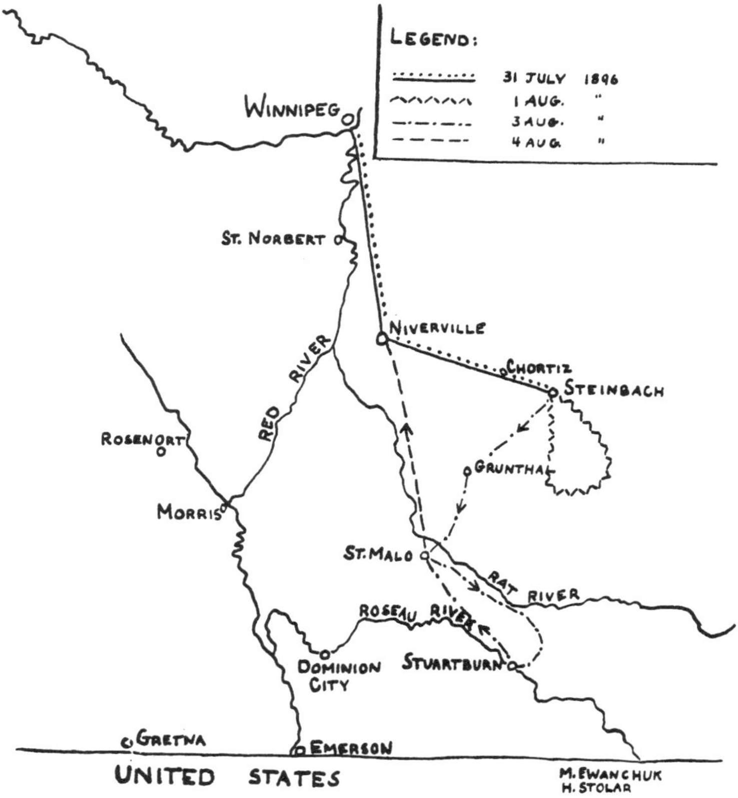

Fig. 1 Map showing the route of the Wendelbo Ukrainian settlers' party, August 1896.

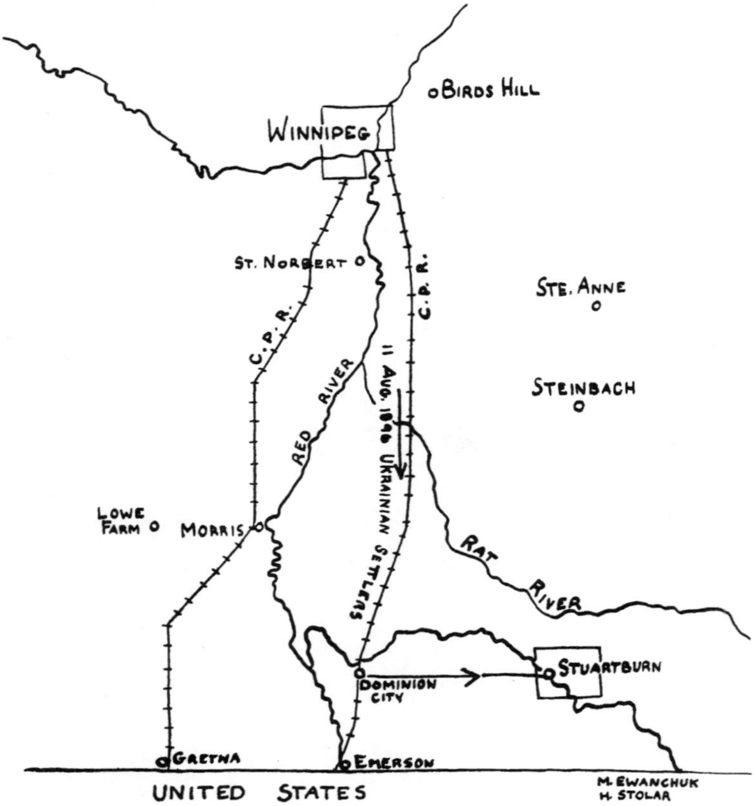

Fig.1a Route of first Oleskiw group.

Chapter 4

The First Group – Pattern of Settlement

The first group organized by Dr. Oleskiw was made up of younger families and eight came as single men. Once the land northeast of the Roseau was surveyed the settlers made entries for their homesteads. Each entry was for a quarter section, 160 acres.

TABLE 1

TABLE 1

List of Original Ukrainian Settlers in the Stuartburn Area and Legal Description of Land Settled.

NAME OF SETTLER		Sec.	Twp.	Rge.	East of 1M.	No. of Souls
Ivan Prygroski (Ivan Prygrocki)	SE¼	22	2	6	E	5
Nykolai Kahut (Nicola Kohut)	NE¼	22	2	6	E	1
Onofry Smuk (Onufry Smuk)	NW¼	22	2	6	E	4
Josef Bzowy	SW¼	28	2	6	E	4
Iwan Storoszuk (Ivan Storoszczuk)	NW¼	28	2	6	E	2
Jan Tomeszewski (Ivan Tomaszewski)	NE¼	28	2	6	E	4
Simon Salamandyk (Semen Salamandyk)	SE¼	28	2	6	E	6
Nikol Wyseczynski (Nicola Wysoczynski)	NW¼	14	2	6	E	1
Wasyl Stefura	SW¼	14	2	6	E	4
Jakob Szelep (Jacob Szelyp)	SE¼	14	2	6	E	1
Iwan Negrycz	NE¼	14	2	6	E	1
Fedor Horobec	NW¼	10	2	6	E	3
Charles Genik (Cyril Genik)	NW¼	16	2	6	E	6
Wasyl Zahara	NW¼	2	2	6	E	6
Maksym Stasyszn	SE¼	10	2	6	E	3
Micheal Prytoski (Michael Prygrocki)	NW¼	12	2	6	E	5
Itasz Prokopczuk (Ilasz Prokopczuk)	NE¼	12	2	6	E	6
Fedor Pidhirny	SW¼	24	2	6	E	5
Wasyl Salamandyk	SE¼	24	2	6	E	3
Ivan Salamandyk	NE¼	24	2	6	E	1
Hehory Prygroski (Hryhory Prygrocki)	SE¼	30	2	6	E	5
Nikol Prygroski (Nicola Prygrocki)	NE¼	30	2	6	E	1
Peter Majkowski	NW¼	20	2	6	E	1
Nikol Majkowski	NE¼	20	2	6	E	1
Sawka Perun	SW¼	30	2	6	E	5
Peter Strurbicki (Peter Strumbicki)	NW¼	30	2	6	E	7
Fedor Dymianyk	NW¼	24	2	6	E	3
						94

A glance at Table 1 will show that the settlers occupied only even numbered sections. This created a patchwork quilt pattern that would present difficulty in the development of roads from the very beginning. This mode of settlement is illustrated in Fig.2. In Fig.2 we also see that Wasyl Zahara who was from a different Province settled the farthest south in NW ¼ Sect. 2.

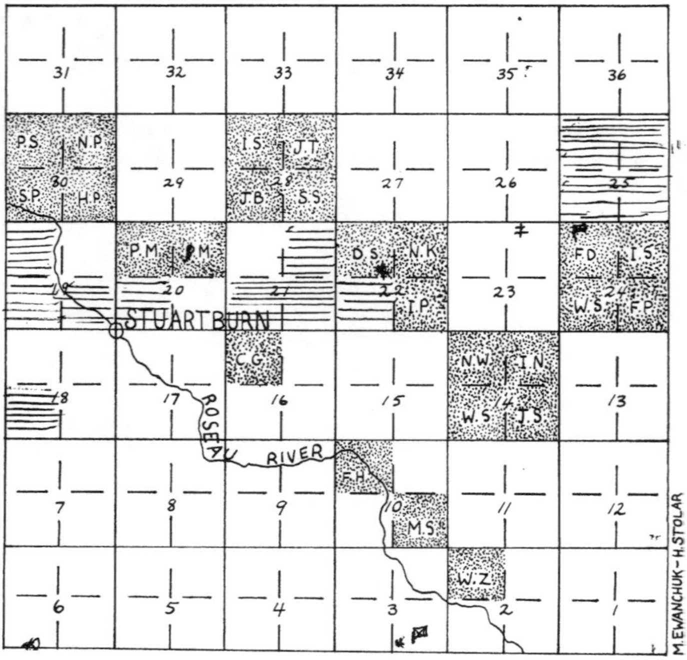

Fig. 2 Homesteads selected by the Oleskiw settlers in Township 2, Range 6, East of the Principal Meridan. (land claimed by Anglo-Saxon settlers)

Fig. 3 Sir Clifford, Minister of the Interior, 1896-1905 (Public Archives of Canada)

Restricting the settlement of the Ukrainians to the even-numbered sections was impractical and unfair. The immigration authorities consequently reacted to this with alacrity bringing it to the attention to the officials at Ottawa and the Minister of the Interior took immediate action to rectify the situation.

410595
Ottawa, 14th April 1897

TO HIS EXCELLENCY
THE GOVERNOR GENERAL IN COUNCIL

The undersigned has the honour to report that a number of settlers are applying for permission to make homestead entry for portions of odd-numbered sections in Township 2, Ranges 6 and 7, East of the First Dominion Lands Meridian. It appears desirable in the public interest that their wishes should be met, and the undersigned accordingly recommends that the odd-numbered sections in the two townships mentioned be opened to homestead entry in so far as the same may be vacant and available.

Respectfully submitted,
(sgd.) Clifford Sipton,
Minister of the Interior.

Hon. Clifford Sifton's letter indicates that the officials recognized that there was no room for land speculation and that the Ukrainians were making such a fine adjustment to Canada. Consequently, the odd-numbered sections were opened to homestead entry, and in 1897 a great increase of Ukrainian settlers arrived. This inflock continued.

PART	SEC.	TP.	RGE.	NAME
NW¼	4	1	6E	Wasyl Maly (Maley)
SE¼	4	1	6E	Kost Dubniak
NW¼	17	1	6E	Fedor Molynek (Malynyk)
SW¼	17	1	6E	Wasyl Kindzierski
SE¼	17	1	6E	Nykola Salomon
NE¼	18	1	6E	Iwan Hudyma
NW¼	18	1	6E	Semen Saranchuk
NE¼	19	1	6E	Tanasko Kostyniuk
SW¼	19	1	6E	Todor Glowacki
NW¼	19	1	6E	Iwan Wiwchar
SE¼	10	1	6E	Iwan Kostyniuk
SE¼	20	1	6E	Yakem Kowaliuk
NE¼	20	1	6E	Petro Hudyma
SW¼	20	1	6E	Iwan Kowaluk
NW¼	20	1	6E	Michal Zahara
NW¼	21	1	6E	Nikolaj Rozka (Roshko)
SW¼	21	1	6E	George Shydlowski
SE¼	21	1	6E	Jakob Zahara
NE¼	21	1	6E	Todor Orlecki
NE¼	22	1	6E	Dmytrash Pauluk
SE¼	22	1	6E	Simion Korol
NW¼	22	1	6E	Aksentyj Dmytruk
SW¼	22	1	6E	Onofrij Tyran (Tyron)
N½—				
NW¼	14	1	6E	Petro Duleniak
SW¼	14	1	6E	Nekola Goszuliak
NE¼	14	1	6E	Wasyl Goszuliak
SW¼	15	1	6E	Achtemij Stefiuk
NW¼	15	1	6E	Danylo Posztar
SE¼	15	1	6E	Iwan Zyha
NE¼	15	1	6E	Dmytro Kosowan
NE¼	16	1	6E	Petro Dzaman
SW¼	16	1	6E	Aksenia Kosowan (widow)
SE¼	16	1	6E	Metro Shewchuk
NE¼	17	1	6E	Petro Salamon
NE¼	28	1	6E	Iwan Bojczuk
SE¼	28	1	6E	Domna Serediuk
SW¼	28	1	6E	Wasyl Shewchuk
Pt.				
NW¼	28	1	6E	Andrij Glowacki
NE¼	30	1	6E	Michalo Wiwsianyk
SE¼	30	1	6E	Wasyl Czornopyski
NW¼	30	1	6E	Elash Kossowan
SW¼	30	1	6E	Onufrij Hryhorasz
SW¼	31	1	6E	Ivon Bojda
SE¼	31	1	6E	Andrij Halicki
NE¼	32	1	6E	Todor Maksymchuk
SW¼	32	1	6E	Nikola Djoba
N½—				
NE¼	33	1	6E	Maksym Malicki

PART	SEC.	TP.	RGE.	NAME
S½—				
NE¼	33	1	6E	Iwan Towstowaryk
NW¼	33	1	6E	Wasyl Chornopyski
SE¼	33	1	6E	Dmytrash Olijnyk
SW¼	33	1	6E	Dmytrash Dutchak
SE¼	23	1	6E	Iwan Marchuk
NW¼	24	1	6E	Wasyl Sidor
NE¼	24	1	6E	Iwan Odokychuk
SW¼	24	1	6E	Nikol Sidor
SW¼	25	1	6E	Semen Badiuk
NE¼	25	1	6E	Iwan Tkadiuk (Badiuk)
SE¼	25	1	6E	George Tkachuk
NE¼	26	1	6E	Iwan Denyshchuk
NW¼	27	1	6E	Dmytro Korol
SE¼	27	1	6E	Sandyk Mekelij
NE¼	27	1	6E	Petro Shkwarchuk
NE¼	2	2	5E	Hrynko Poloz
NW¼	2	2	5E	Michal Panisiak
SE¼	2	2	5E	Hrynko Shmyr
SW¼	2	2	5E	Wasyl Gushczak
SE¼	3	2	5E	Ilo German
NE¼	3	2	5E	Iwan Nykolajishyn
SE¼	4	2	5E	Tomko Federczuk
SE¼	5	2	5E	Danylo Struzowski
NE¼	10	2	5E	Olesko Tkaczuk
L.S. 7 & 8 of				
SE¼	10	2	5E	Fedor Czubej
NE¼	12	2	5E	Fedor Horobec
NW¼	12	2	5E	Iwan German
SW¼	12	2	5E	John Jaremovich
NW¼	13	2	5E	Stefan Horbul
SE¼	13	2	5E	Michal Kaminski
NE¼	13	2	5E	Dymian Horbul
SW¼	13	2	5E	Michal Horbul
NE¼	34	1	6E	Wasyl Roshka
SE¼	34	1	6E	Iwan Hrynyk
N½—				
NW¼	34	1	6E	Gawrylo Kantymir
S½—				
NW¼	34	1	6E	Ivon Woroniuk
SE¼	35	1	6E	Achtemij Miszczanczuk
L.S. 3 & 4 of				
SW	35	1	6E	John Golecki
L.S. 5 & 6 of				
SW	35	1	6E	Jan Szczygelski
SE¼	19	1	7E	Iwan Tkachuk
NE¼	19	1	7E	Iwan Kowaliuk
SE¼	32	1	7E	Jakiw Niwranski
NE¼	32	1	7E	Dmytro Niwranski
NE¼	1	2	5E	Josef Bzowy
NW¼	1	2	5E	Stach Lepeshchak
SW¼	1	2	5E	Marcin Lepishchuk

Fig. 4 List of early settlers.

Part II
First Oleskiw Settlement in Manitoba

Chapter 1

The Settling of the Canadian West

It was during the last year of Prime Minister John A. Macdonald's term in office that Dr. Joseph Oleskiw arrived in Canada to investigate the opportunities for the land-hungry Ukrainian peasants for settling in Canada. There was great agitation among the Ukrainians to escape the repressive Romanoff and Hapsburg rulers. And it was Rev. Iwan Wolanski who, on investigating the fate of the Ukrainians who went to Brazil, dissuaded further immigration to that country. Acting, therefore, on the information received from Rev. Wolanski, Dr. J. Oleskiw came to Canada in 1895.

In 1896 the Sir Wilfred Laurier government assumed leadership in Canada and on a 35-year-old Minister of the Interior, Clifford Sifton, fell the task for the establishment of a workable policy for the settlement of Western Canada.

True, before 1896 settlers from Ontario and the Maritimes came to the west, but did they stay? No.

The Times of Winnipeg reported on the situation as follows:

> The trails from Manitoba to the States were worn bare by the footprints of departing settlers[1]

Consequently:

> When Clifford Sifton was appointed minister responsible for immigration in 1896, he inherited a badly managed department that was incapable of attracting the kind of immigrants required to build Canada's West. Indeed, prior to Sifton taking office, the Prairies had suffered a population loss.
>
> The Liberal MP from Manitoba quickly went about setting things right. He streamlined departmental bureaucracy, introduced changes to make more land available for settlers, promoted the West as a land of unlimited opportunity and increased the budget for overseas promotion and recruitment.
>
> He also did something else. He made sure Canada recruited people with the skill and desire to come to the Prairies and stay.[2]

Sir Clifford Sifton had his immigration officers accept the credo: that the settlers were customers and the customer is always right[3]

---

1 Vidi, The Winnipeg Free Press, December 7, 1997, p. B4.
2 The Winnipeg Free Press, November 27, 1997.
3 Vidi, J. W. Defoe, Clifford Sifton in Relation to his Times.

To start with, Anglo-Saxon settlers south west of the Roseau River did accept the Ukrainian settlers of 1896, and a few years following, as customers. To them they provided transportation to the homesteads; their business men of Dominion City sold food and clothing – their business increased. The farmers, too were able to find a ready market for their surplus cows, oxen, swine and poultry, as well as seed grain.

The Ukrainians who came were genuine settlers; regrettably, they settled on swampy waste lands east of the Roseau. They came, they settled on homesteads and they stayed. Such, however, was not the case with others. Even some Icelanders of 1874 left for North Dakota.

The Ukrainians were determined to stay and do well and of the 1903 and 1904 settlers most of them remained.

The Ukrainian group that settled in the Stuartburn "colony" tried to establish neighborly relations with the settlers to the south west of them.

But there was still some unoccupied railway land. Other quarters and sections were acquired by Anglo-Saxons even before 1880. It would be unfair to impute that this acquisition was done specifically in anticipation of the coming of Ukrainians except, maybe, in cases like that of Franklin Henry, who somehow laid claim to large tracts in 1903. There was also the case of Richard Foley who was an immigration agent in the Interlake area and who had land there and even had a post office named after him. He laid claim to some quarters.

There was a fairly large Anglo-Saxon colony south of Dominion City and at the start relations between the two groups, juxta posed on each side of the Roseau were tolerable, but this did not last. Some exploitation of the people who knew not the English language began to develop; for instance, a settler from the west contracted to buy seasoned poplar poles for fuel from a Ukrainian at 75 cents a load. When he arrived, however, he had a four-horse team hitched to a sleigh with eight foot bunks, instead of four, and drove away with the equal of four loads for 75 cents. The Ukrainian settler considered this to be unfair and, consequently, resented the lack of good will; and when similar transactions took place the line dividing the two groups became more firm.

Chapter 2

Homestead Settlement

When the two delegates from the village of Senkiw went to Lviv to get first hand information about Canada from Prof. Joseph Oleskiw (to repeat) he made one suggestion: take with you all possible trade tools that may help establish a manufacturing industry and hand tools for building and the cultivation of land. The settlers' trunks were full of tools to start farming, and there were tradesmen among them. Consequently, the shoemaker brought his last, the weaver several shuttles, the cabinet maker tools of his specialty and the "master-builders" came with hatchets, broad axes, planes, chisels, hammers, squares and various types of saws, yes, and a wooden square, "vincle". Then in trunks and packing cases were packed hoes, cradles, scythes and spades.

The women, on the other hand, brought some cooking utensils, and cutlery. But most importantly they brought tiny bundles of seed to be able to start a garden, flower seeds, too. They were prepared to live off the land.

However, once the people selected their homesteads they had to start the building of living accommodation – a home of some type. One thing the homesteaders lacked - if they had suitable logs on their land - was horses or oxen to draw them to the building site. Men, though, helped each other and carried logs on their backs. Fortunately the logs in the area were not big.

The Manitoba agronomist, K. S. Prodan, left information about the early home building after he interviewed many of the original pioneers. One of them was Theodosy Wachna who stated:

> Those were difficult days: As soon as the settlers selected their farms, those who were able started to build a house in order that his family may have a place to live in. Some lived in rented quarters for a while. Houses were built out of poplar logs as no other timber grew here. Those logs were not very huge as fires used to pass through this area very often. Actually now the poplar trees are much larger...The roofs were thatched with reeds which were in plentiful supply. Where reeds were not available the thatch was made of hay...Nearly all built their homes in which they could live a long time. There were also some temporary buildings.
>
> In July of 1897 the then Immigration Commissioner, McCreary in Winnipeg hired me as an immigration agent. His purpose was that I would act as guide to some 30 Ukrainian families and help them settle in the Stuartburn area. All the family groups assigned to this area arrived and settled in Township 1 and Range 5 in the vicinity of the present hamlet of Tolstoi. The following arrived at that time: Kost Mandzj, Samuel Pudkowski, Tkachyks, Kylyks, Bednars, Lipischak, and others...The homestead land was surveyed and each head of a family tried to select a farm for himself.[1]

Michael Stashyn recorded the building of the first accommodation by his parents.

---

1 K. S. Prodan, THE LEADER, Winnipeg, 1931, p.35

Theodore Wachna was eighteen years old when he came to Scranton Pa. In 1892.

In 1896 he came to Stuartburn.

In the U.S.A. he attended night school and learned English.

THE FIRST HOUSE

Soon it was imperative to build a house as winter was approaching. But how was this to be done? Nykola Genik saved the situation. At one time he had lived in the Carpathian mountains and knew how to build "huts". He showed us how to do this and helped us to build a home. It was some home! We excavated a basement about three feet deep. At each end of the excavation we dug in a post and placed a beam to connect the two of them. On each side we leaned poles against the beam to constitute a wall. The poles were covered with turf and soil. One gable was plastered with mud in which a 10 x 10 inch window pane was set in. This was our window. The second gable had a door, made of hewn poles. It was a great holiday when we had our new home. There was great joy and happiness! The ledges between the basement wall and the lower part of the leaning wall served us for beds. Somewhere we found an ink bottle which served as an oil receptacle for our lamp...We used to make the wicks for this lamp out of the available thread.

To heat the cabin, "kulyba" a peech (stove) was made of clay and stones. (Some did acquire a box stove) The floor was made of puddled-clay and when dry was covered with hay. Such a dwelling proved adequate for temporary shelter.

These homes provided shelter, not only for the homesteader himself, but also other families and some single men. Very often the "kulybas" were fully thatched.

The "kulyba" type was erected to shelter the family while the homestead homes were built. Those described by Michael Stashyn had better finished roofs.

Though some people built cabins out of available seasoned poplars, mud-plastered them and made a roof of sod and hay bundles (Fig.1) others managed to find an adequate supply of fair-sized logs to erect homes of a more permanent nature.

Fig. 1 Senkiw home, 1905 Built by Peter Smuk.

The settlers either acquired draught animals (oxen) early or were able to get adequate "man-power" to bring logs close to the building site. Others delayed until they would be able to procure good building material from the eastern regions, and build temporary shelters.

In time better types of homes were built. They served for many years. Eventually some even had the outdoor walls finished with siding.

Fig.2 and 3 are examples of better homes after the settlers got established.

Fig. 2

Fig. 3

Recording the progress made by the first Oleskiw group an immigration agent stated:

> These 146 families have cheap, but very comfortable houses. Their building improvements on each place are worth at an average about $50.00 Plenty of hay put up for their stock. The growing crop is good, and seems well put in, except the potatoes that are poor. Plenty of work to be had in the neighborhood of the settlement, and they ought to be able to make enough to support themselves during the coming winter.

Nevertheless, as winter approached some settlers were running short of finances to support their families through the winter.

Fig. 4 First Reaping

Chapter 3

Difficulties of Getting Started

Once the settlers provided themselves with shelter they started clearing land to be able to seed grain and plant vegetables. They cleared small patches of land and with hoe and spade and prepared the virgin soil for planting in the spring.

Most of the 1896 group of settlers arrived too late to plant vegetables or grain, but were able to seed fall rye and fall wheat with seed which they brought with them or acquired to the Anglo-Saxon farmer. Grain was planted by hand by being broadcast. Hand seeding required fine skill and produced good results.

In 1897 in small patches of wheat, oats, barley, buckwheat and corn were planted. Millet was also sown: They came prepared to till the soil and live off the land.

In crates they brought, one would find: a spade, a hoe, a scythe, a sickle or two, a flail and a sieve. During the first winter men fashioned cradles for cutting grain and vessels - scoops made of wood for winnowing . Rakes were made by using the willow crotch for a handle. In some instances willow crotches were also employed as forks.

Willing and able as they were to commence farming, when the winter of 1896 set in, some were short of supplies. Those who had money were able to acquire staples in Dominion City and small items in Houle's store, but they were short of vegetables.

Settlers with available means bought cows, swine and hens from the farmers to the west. Some even acquired a yoke of oxen. This was a great 'boon' to the Anglo-Saxon farmers and they were glad the Ukrainian settlers came.

Nonetheless, some settlers had sold their all in the Old Country, and after paying for transportation from Ukraine to Winnipeg, found themselves short of money to provide food for the family.

The Settlers were Fortunate

In the first place they were fortunate thanks to Dr. Joseph Oleskiw's foresight in selecting Kyrilo Genik to be in charge of the group that came, for he soon acquired enough knowledge of English to convey the needs of the settlers to the officials. In the second place, they were fortunate due to the favourable attitude of the immigration agents.

Michael Stashyn recorded that one day a man in a fur coat came around, and somehow was able to write down the needs of the people. At that time the Stashyn family was living in a "kulyba". This visit provided results. The agent, Mr. Carstens, took action and as "some needed assistance ...and were supplied with flour and cornmeal,"...18 heads of families are willing to go to work at anything." (Carstens)[1]

1 (pp 380647) Hugo Carstens.

This indicates that governmental officials continued to pay heed to insure that the settlers were not in need during the winter months. The supplies the settlers received were mainly flour and cornmeal. The cost of these supplies were eventually entered against the homesteads of individual settlers. The listing that follows shows the cost of supplies at two stores in Dominion City.

Price of flour and cornmeal in Dominion City:

Agrew and Co:	flour xxxx	$1.15 per sack
	cornmeal	$1.90
Marshall & Scott:	flour xxxx	$1.35 per each
	cornmeal	$1.95

(Flour and cornmeal were from the Emerson mill.)

The Stuartburn postmaster, Ramsey offered to deliver goods at 15¢ per cwt., and James Simpson at 20¢ per cwt. (In 1896 and 1897 a total of $341.55 was spent in assistance.)

It must be noted that even in 1896 some men and boys went harvesting and earned the much needed cash, which in some cases was spent in buying cows and piglets.

After the first group arrived, others followed. Unfortunately they were coming too late in the season, and were facing the winter without shelter, supplies and employment. The first group, nevertheless, had made progress:

> There are at present 31 families: 16 families settled in the latter part of August; 4 in October and 8 in November; 21 families have no stock; others had 34 head of cattle; those who did not erect shelter live with others.[2]

Hugo Carstens also observed that:

> While in Dominion City my attention was drawn to the need of some accommodation for new arrivals and for the convenience of those who came 25 miles to shop in Dominion City.[3]

The attitude continued favourable.

Life places certain demands on people forming a new settlement. Such a demand was faced by all settlers in the west. This demand was to set aside land for a cemetery. This the Oleskiw settlers east of Stuartburn did by setting a piece of land along the trail between Stuartburn and the Shevchenko district to the east. And it was done in this manner: each settler gave a parcel of land and a cemetery became available, but it was in the middle of the section.

2 Ibid to H. H. Smith, December 7, 1896.
3 Ibid.

Iwan Machnij (Machnee)

When news from Wasyl Zahara reached Bridok that he was well established on 113 morgens of land for which he paid ten dollars, people in the Province of Bukovina began to make plans to emigrate to Canada, and one of them was Iwan Machnij. It was 1897 when the Machnij family left Chernivtski. They arrived in Dominion City and on March 6, 1897 he was on his homestead after spending four days with the Zaharas. He was a carpenter by trade and immediately went to work to build a log and sod cabin to house his family of five children. Mrs. Machnij, of course wanted to help carrying the logs to the cabin site, unfortunately, however, in lifting a heavy log, she ruptured herself. Nevertheless, undaunted by her infirmity she tied a heavy shawl around her waist and resumed her work: the children needed shelter.

The Machnij located on the southwest quarter Sec 5-2-6E west of Purple Bank school. It wasn't a very good quarter - too many stones and the soil was light. Sanchira Machnij (nee Tyron) dug a garden and planted vegetables. And when Mr. Iwan Machnij went harvesting she took care of the homestead and managed to earn enough to buy groceries by digging Seneca roots. When they arrived in Canada, there were five children in the family: Georgi 11, Michael 9, Anetzka 4, Waselyna 3, and Maria 1. The older children took care of the younger ones and the baby.

Sanchira died after a two-year illness and Iwan soon remarried when a widow, Paraskeva Hudyma arrived from Bridok with two children: the family increased. Paraskeva was only thirty years old and the second marriage increased the family size further. According to Gerald Machnee the farm is still in the family's hands (Iwan Machnij also Machnee). Gerald was one that became a graduate of the University of Manitoba and was employed as a meteorologist.

Iwan Machnij was forty years old when he came to the Stuartburn-Gardenton area. He passed to his reward in 1949 after having given a half century of his busy and devoted pioneer life to Canada. He was laid to rest in the St. Michael's cemetery.[4]

Fig. 4 Iwan Machnee family in 1906

4 Information gleaned from the Machnee family history.

Chapter 4

Earlier Land Acquisition East of the Red

Even before the arrival of the Ukrainian settlers in 1896, there were attempts to acquire land in the corner of the province, north of the 49th and east of the Red, in anticipation of future development of the area. Sir R. J. Cartwright, for instance, held claim to a larger acreage than others. In 1880 he acquired 160 acres in 17-2-06; 344 acres in 19-02-06; 400 acres in 23-01-06 and in 1893, 311 acres in 19-02-06: a total of 1215 acres. This wasn't done in anticipation of the Ukrainians coming, but appears to have been sheer speculation anticipating block settlements of people from the Ontario back-woods.

It must be stressed that Sir R. J. Cartwright was no fly-by-night speculator; he was a very capable man, as may be deduced form the following:

> After the 1896 general election, Wilfred Laurier replaced John A. Macdonald as Prime Minister and selected one of the strongest cabinets in Canadian history, "The Ministry of Talents" as contemporaries described it. It included the redoubtable and experienced Richard Cartwright.[1]

It appears, however, that he wasn't too well informed about the suitability of the land for development as a grain-growing region.

There were others who acquired land, too, among them was Rev. Samuel P. Matheson, who on 20 March 1880 purchased the NW¼ Sec 33, Tp.1, R1E. The cost of this land was $170.55 and he paid down $17.06 and on 22 October 1981 he paid $26.27; then he was in default of further payments and the quarter section was granted as homestead to Jacob Arseny on 17 June 1898.

Nevertheless, an earlier settlement was established between the Roseau River and the Red. This was better land than the area northeast of the Roseau. According to W. J. Sisler's records these settlers came after 1885.

First English-Speaking Group

> Some people, it seems, settled in this area after the Rebellion of 1885. There is a list of 30 families who came in shortly after this – every one with an English, Dutch or Scottish name: "Johnson, Beckett, Post, Marshall, Watting, Whitworth, Read, Vaughan, Connery, Drew, Leith, Knowles, Roso, Fitzgerald, Young, Hamlin, King, McGee, Ramsey, Alcock, Guernsey, Yeo, Smith, Darling, Dodds, Casselman, Robinson, Davis, Roy, Morley, of all these only Johnsons and Millers are left."
>
> There were no roads between Dominion City and the present Stuartburn. It was 20 miles from a market. Many, consequently, threw up their homesteads; others, however, waited longer and when the Ukrainian and a few Icelandic settlers came in to take homesteads east of them, they were glad to sell out.

---

1 Moir & Farr, The Canadian Experience, Ryerson Press, 1969, p.319

The Ukrainians came in 1896 to establish their first block settlement in the Stuartburn area. It appears that before their arrival the settlement of English speaking people in the area terminated abruptly. In addition to W. J. Sisler's list there was also one Frenchman, Houle by name, who had a small store and a post office.

Settlement Problems Continue

Some of the Anglo-Saxon settlers and others due west of Stuartburn got engaged in ranching – pasturage was good and there was an open run to the Roseau River where good water was available. However, it appears, that they were unable to prepare enough fodder for winter feeding and as Rev. Nestor Dmytriw observed after his first visit to the colony the cattle were in very poor condition – likely under-nourished during the winter months.

Some of the Ukrainian settlers selected land west of the Roseau, as was the case with one Nykola Humeniuk. He built a home on the NW¼ of 19-T2-R6E and went to work leaving his wife with two children to fend on their own.

One afternoon at about five o'clock while Mrs. Humeniuk was digging Seneca roots, she smelt smoke: She panicked:

> One Wednesday afternoon I was digging roots close to the house. All at once I noticed a fire to the west. You know how tall and dry the grass is in the autumn of the year. Who knows how the fire started, but once it starts in the grassy area it can move quickly into the bushland where there are many old, dry trees, and dry grass to burn. Soon this fire develops into a conflagration. This had led to the burning of several houses this autumn. I climbed up a ladder to reach the roof of our house and noticed a thick cloud of smoke, about a mile to the west of our home. I descended quickly, took the household effects and carried them to that excavation that was covered with sod. I covered the entrance with other sod and I dug that hurriedly with a spade. But I could not carry out the trunk by myself. Then I took Peter in my arms and carried him across the river, and there I tied him to a tree with a rope that I brought with me and told him not be afraid and not to cry.
>
> You know how cold the water is during the fall of the year but I had to recross the river and pick up Fred and one pillow. By this time I was soaked above my waist and carrying the pillow and one of the boys, I went to spend the night at Hryhorij Prygrocki's home.

Fortunately before she reached her neighbor's home a heavy rain started to fall and stopped the fire from advancing; nevertheless, many haystacks and at least two homes were burnt down.

Whether the new settlers were justified or not, they considered that the fires that destroyed homes on the west side of the Roseau River were set deliberately by the ranchers who wanted to force the new settlers to move to the east side of the Roseau River.

What, however, added credence to the suspicion was the fact that in

October, 1899 N. Humeniuk received notice from the Dominion Land Office in Winnipeg that due to some error in registry he was living on the wrong homestead. It was suggested that he take a good look at NW½ of Section 8, Twp 2., Rge. 6E.[2]

Consequently, the Humeniuks moved to the new homestead in 1899. It was 1¼ south of Stuartburn, leaving a house, a root-cellar and a garden behind, to start from scratch, and all because as:

> Official records show that one rancher wanted the quarter we lived on for the convenience of having access to the river.[3]

There truly was hardship in making progress. Fortunately, the new homestead was a better quarter of land.

Regrettably, subsequently during a dry year a fire that was started west of the Roseau jumped the river and the west wind moved it east burning off the top humus soil and leaving only sandy soil and stones.

---

2 Peter Humeniuk, Hardships and Progress of Ukrainian Pioneers, Peter Humeniuk, Publisher, Derksen Printers, 1977, p.75

3 Ibid.

Chapter 5

Reverend Nestor Dmytriw

In the development and settlement of Canada, the French clergy and the clergy of the English churches played an important role in looking after the spiritual needs of their people, and in the west, encouraging the settlers who were making a start as farmers.

As far as Canadians of Ukrainian extraction were concerned, they should be justly proud of two clergymen: Rev. Iwan Wolanski who helped divert the immigration tide of Ukrainians from Brazil to Canada, and Rev. Nestor Dmytriw the first Ukrainian clergyman to come to the prairies. Both were Ukrainian Catholics, but it was Rev. Nestor Dmytriw who encouraged the Ukrainian Orthodox from Bukovyna and Ukrainian Catholics from Halychyna to work together. He discouraged Polonization and Russi-fiction efforts and his suggestions were taken seriously. During his visits to the first colony at Stuartburn he encouraged the settlers to make a good start on their homesteads.

Reverend Nestor Dmytriw's Visit, 1897

The Ukrainians had barely been in the Stuartburn colony for eight months when they received news that Reverend Nestor Dmytriw would visit them. Before coming to Stuartburn, he visited the Ukrainians settlers in Alberta and the Drifting River (Wasyl Ksionzek group) settlement.

Being an editor of the American Ukrainian paper, "Svoboda"[1], Reverend Nestor Dmytriw was a good writer, but some of his observations tended to contain a considerable tinge of romanticism.

He commenced his report as follows:

> This is the largest Ukrainian colony in Manitoba…I left for this colony on April 16, (1897), leaving Winnipeg at 8 o'clock in the morning. With me on the train there was one family…and two residents (from Stuartburn) who walked a distance of 54 miles to meet their countrymen. It is important to know that there is a separate class of coach car with wooden seats for the accommodation of the immigrants. I sat among our people and enquired in detail about everything that I needed to know.
>
> I arrived in Dominion City. The postman from Stuartburn took me on his wagon and I settled down comfortably being seated on bags of flour which he was delivering for our people, and we travelled slowly a distance of some 20 miles. The Englishman whistled as we rode along and the horses walked at a reasonable pace, and I got very cold from the wind that blew from the north. It seemed to carry the cold it absorbed from the frozen swamps. By night fall, we arrived at our destination and I was accommodated in a most welcome manner in the home of Mr. Peter Mykowsky[2]; I wish at this time to express my sincere thanks and appreciation to him for the warm welcome.

---

1 Rev. Nestor Dmytriw, Svoboda 1897.

2 Peter Maykowsky was a progressive settler who had the money to erect a house about a half mile north of Houle's store. He later returned to Ukraine.

Trip from Dominion City to Stuartburn

Fig. 1 Reverend Iwan Wolanski

Fig. 2 Reverend Nestor Dmytriw, 1895 (Photo courtesy Svoboda)

The next day after arrival, Reverend Dmytriw started to visit the farmers. The first farm visited, he recorded, had buildings very much of a temporary nature.

> The second farm I visited was that of a wealthier man. The house was spacious like that of a well-to-do farmer in Western Ukraine, his farm buildings were well kept. In the farmyard there was a wagon costing $60, a plough and in the stable there were four oxen, two cows and a calf. Back of the house there is a ploughed field and past it, a bluff clear of underbrush. It is pleasant to look at such a farmyard. This man brought $500 in cash with him and with the help of his three sons is busily engaged in developing his property. I feel certain that within five years he will outstrip the English and German farmers who settled here earlier, and this goes without says as far as the French are concerned.

The third settler complained about being poor because before he left the German landlord and the Jewish innkeeper extorted from him most of the available money.

> Our settler, however, does not sit idle with folded hands. In spite of heavy frosts, he cuts down trees to build a house, even though it be a humble cabin, but he has built it himself and lives in it, in the hope that: "at least it will be easier for my children here..."
>
> ...And really it is a pleasure to see what colossal progress our children are making...The younger children are going to school and learning the English language.

In order to appraise what progress was possible, Reverend Dmytriw also visited the home of an English farmer and observed that after seven years he had erected a modern house which was well furnished and had a piano for his girl. His house was in very good condition, but his cattle, more than 30 head had:

> ...come through the winter in such a poor condition that it is pitiful to look at them. The farm machinery and various types of equipment are left out to rust in the farmyard; however, the horses, on the other hand, are exceptionally well fed. I feel that in seven years time the Ukrainian settler will show much better progress that the English farmer was able to attain.

The Ukrainians were to celebrate Palm Sunday on the 18th of April 1897. In readiness for an open air service about a mile and a half east of Houle's store, they erected a cross and made an altar.

> They rejoiced that on Sunday they would have a large procession and celebrate Palm Sunday. Regrettably, however, a storm blew up during the night. There was thunder and lightning and toward morning the snow began to fall...The storm increased and the snow was whirled around by a frigid northern wind...It was such a bitterly cold winter day that Sunday, a day the like of which I had never before experienced in my life. You could feel the frigid wind cutting the flesh to the bone. It was impossible to get warm. All of us, though stiffened by the cold, managed to reach the store where I sang Mass and confessed 87 people. Many, however, due to the bitter cold did not come.

Before departing, the dedicated missionary summarized his observations:

- 24 families settled in 1896 and others came in the fall and additional settlers arrived;
- land is generally good, but has too many stones;
- there are excellent meadows;
- all kinds of cereals and vegetables grow in the area;
- suitable country for raising cattle;
- employment available south of the border during harvest season;
- from some of the people I did get the impression that life is more difficult for them in Canada than it would be in the Ukraine and
- the people need a church and land for a (married) clergyman so that he could support himself.

On Monday, April 19 he left by wagon for Dominion City where he met more Ukrainians who arrived from Winnipeg on their way to the Stuartburn colony.[3]

Rev. Nestor Dmytriw Government Immigration Agent

Rev. Nestor Dmytriw was most concerned over the dishonest actions of some German agents and their associates luring and arranging for many

3 Reverend Nestor Dmytriw's visit is translated and based on his repast in Svoboda, and republished by UVAN in Winnipeg, M. H. Marunchak, editor.

poor settlers to go under contract to Georgia and Hawaii, who in time penniless and discouraged were making their way to Canada (those from Georgia he mentions in particular). That aspect of the mass migration called for closer research. It was the unscrupulous agents who recruited settlers with small means and without suitable protection on the way, they were further "stripped" and arrived in the prairie penniless depending on the good will of other settlers who were financially secure.

Yes, the officials of the Canadian Government of the day depended on German agents and German steamship companies when bringing settlers from Europe; they did not accept Dr. Oleskiw's plan. Pierre Berton rightly observes:

> Oleskiw grew dejected. His pamphlet extolling the Canadian West, describing his tour of the prairies and giving practical advice to would-be emigrants, was read by thousands. But, it was the shipping agents who reaped the benefit. They slipped into villages, disguised as pedlars and itinerant journeymen, signed up anybody they could promise the moon, and cheated their victims.

As Superintendent of Immigration, Rev. Nestor Dmytriw also warned the government about the work of German agents. And in September 1897, one such agent Ignatius Roth even travelled to the Stuartburn colony to investigate the progress Oleskiw's settlers were making to use them as an example of success to induce others to come.

Rev. Nestor Dmytriw and Alfred Aberlindth

Alfred Aberlindth and Rev. Nestor Dmytriw met two trains filled to capacity with new immigrants, most from western Ukraine, but for some reason Rev. Dmytriw refused to supervise the first train. Aberlindth reports on his train.

> There were 462 souls of which 315 bought tickets, the rest were children in mother's arms.
>
> - They carried around $11,000 in cash
>
> - Their destinations were:
> Edmonton, 78; Dauphin, 90; Pleasant Home, 15; Dominion City 17, Brokenhead 28, Yorkton 47 and Saltcoats 29.
>
> - In Montreal they bought 350 loaves of rye bread, and more was bought in Ottawa
>
> - Enroute they were met by Mr. McCreary and his Jewish translator
>
> - When they left Rat Portage (Kenora) more bread was bought and given to the people. Dr. English found one child ill with measles.
>
> - Due to the fact that there was an Exhibition in Winnipeg the trains were shunted to Stony Mountain with all the passengers except twenty Germans who travelled in the tourist section.

- Most of the people who arrived were in good physical condition.

- Records show that through the early years 22 Icelanders, 366 Jews, 566 Poles and 350 Ukrainians without means and with physical problems were deported.

The large number of Ukrainians deported was due to the fact that Mike Murowec and Co., the German agents campaigned in Western Ukraine and brought in large numbers of poor people, and those whom they managed to bring in bypassing strict medical examinations.

In Halifax, those Ukrainians being deported pleaded with Rev. Nestor Dmytriw for help. It was beyond his ability to help them.

The situation drove him to distraction. The seriousness of the situation about which he and Dr. Oleskiw expressed concern and warned the governmental officials were finally underscored by F. W. McCreary. He reported:

> ...upon examination, corroborated by my previous suspicions that they were induced to emigrate although in a destitute condition by a promise of a Shipping Agent, Mr. Michael Moravec of Hamburg who distinctly promised them not only free land but that the Canadian Government would further assist them by grants for subsistence, by gifts of cattle and tools. Were such shamefully dishonest practices exposed in the proper manner by officials in Hamburg and elsewhere, the results would be very beneficial.[4]

However, Rev. Dmytriw's duties were too demanding. Therefore, after falling ill in Winnipeg, he terminated his services and returned to the U.S.A. There is no evidence to show that he ever returned to visit in Canada.

4 F. W. McCreary to James A. Smart, Deputy of Immigration, P.A.C. 38073.

Fig. 3 Ukrainian immigrants.

Chapter 6

Settlement Pattern to the Southeast

Most quarters in 2-6 east of the present hamlet of Stuartburn were open as homesteads, but land in T-1 R-5 seemed to have been acquired by Anglo-Saxons and others. The 1896 group and those who followed settled in T2 R6. Then came settlers from the Zahara's area who settled on land south of the present hamlet of Gardenton.

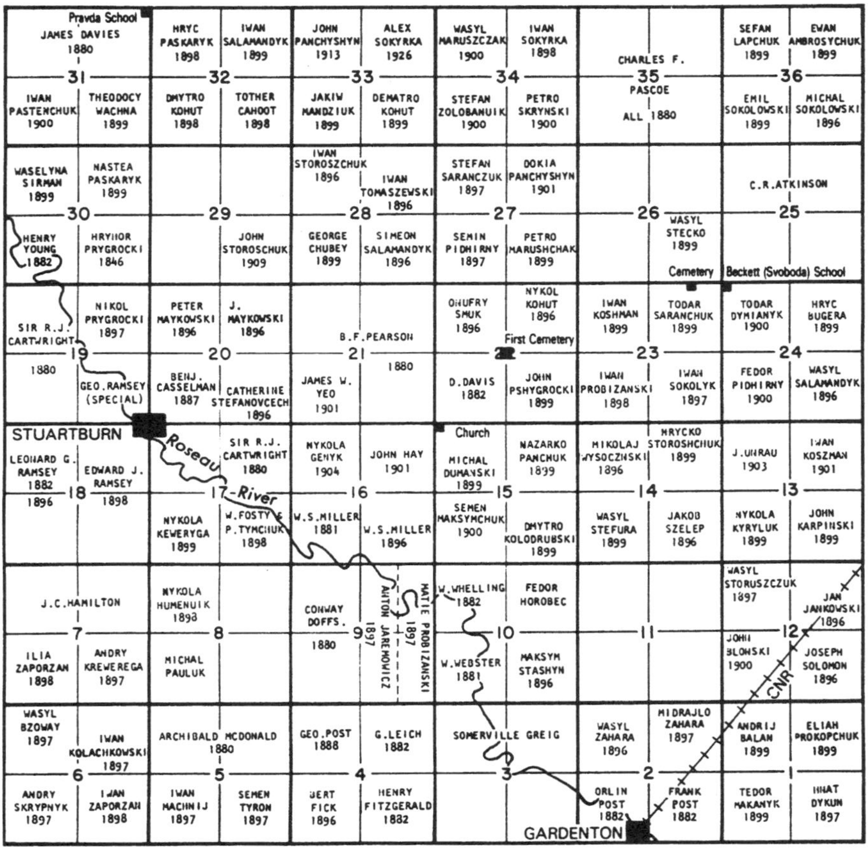

Fig. 1 Note: There were several quarter sections claimed by Anglo-Saxons

Gardenton Area

The solid Ukrainian group that came from the region south of the Dnister River in the province of Bukovyna, though ethnically related to the people of the Senkiw and Boschiv regions north of the Dnister differed in matters of religion and formed a separate community. They were adherents of the Greek Orthodox Church, whereas the Senkiw group settlers were Greek Catholics.

Southwest of Gardenton the parish of St. Michaels was eventually organized. The new settlers took up land to the southeast between the Roseau River and the 49th parallel, fanned out to the Icelandic settlement of Arbakka. This area had inferior agricultural land that they soon called, "the prairie"- it was low grassland with hardly any trees. Their wood supply and building material came from the banks of the Roseau. However, the large timber was denuded by Sprague Lumber Company and floated to sawmills in Winnipeg.

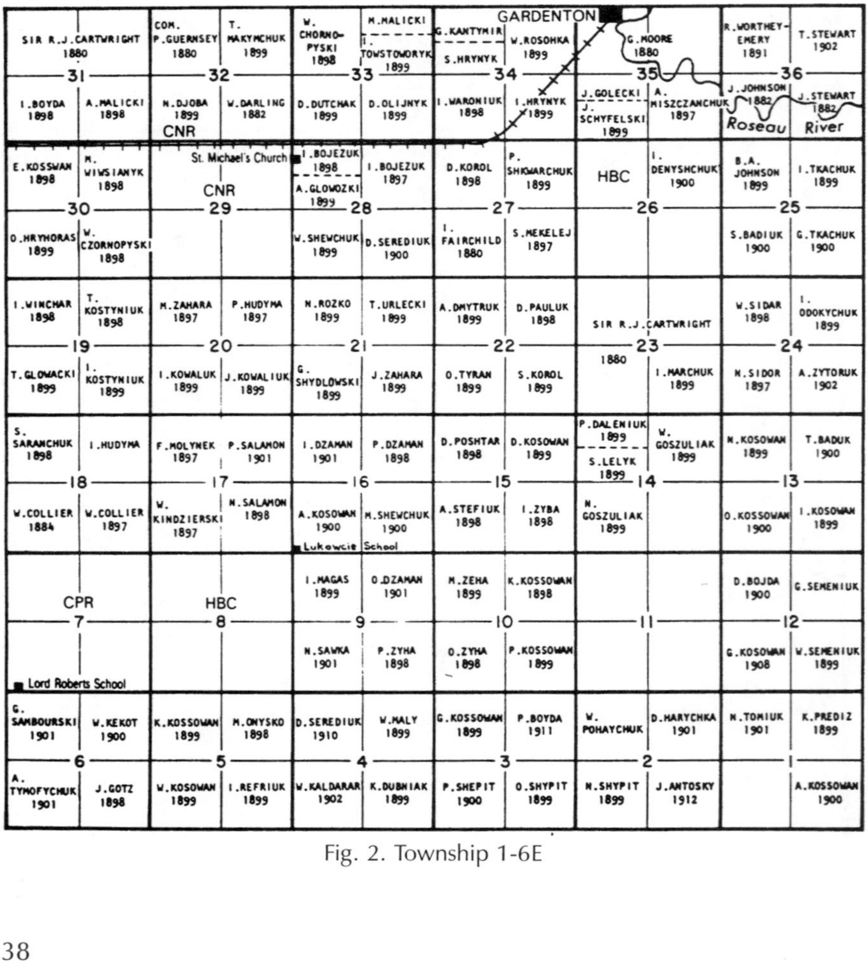

Fig. 2. Township 1-6E

Tolstoi Settlers

In 1897, as more settlers arrived they were directed to the lands to the south and to the west of the present hamlet of Tolstoi – west toward Overstone, and south toward the border.

> We have this information recorded from an interview with Theodosy Wachna: In July of 1897 the then Immigration Commissioner, McCreary in Winnipeg hired me as an immigration agent. His purpose was that I would act as guide to some 30 Ukrainian families and help them settle in the Stuartburn area. All the family groups assigned to this area arrived and settled in Township 1 and Range 5 in the vicinity of the present hamlet of Tolstoi. The following arrived at that time: Kost Mandzj, Samuel Pudkowski, Tkachyks, Kylyks, Bednars, Lipischak, and others...The homestead land was surveyed and each head of a family tried to select a farm for himself.[1]

From a letter received from Maurice Kalushka we learn that some settlers even came into the Tolstoi region via Georgia and Chicago. He provided us with the following information about his grandfather Hnat Galushka who settled on SW½ 22T1 R5E.

Hnat Galushka

My grandfather, Hnat Galushka, was born in 1858 in a village called Cebriw in the western Ukraine. At an early age he married Ewdokia Brelinski. He was the son of a well-to-do landowner, lands which his father acquired during the partition of lands following the abolition of the feudal system (panschyna) in 1848.

In 1896 he emigrated with his wife and four children, Annie, Katherine, Peter and Barbara along with a few other families, to the state of Georgia and settled near Jackson.

Their original destination was Canada but due to some misrepresentation on the passports by an agent they did not arrive in Canada where his sister, married to Onufrey Kudryk, father of the well-known Rev. Wasyl Kudryk had taken up a homestead near what later became known as Tolstoi. The post office at the time was called Oleksiw.

After eleven months in Georgia the family moved to Chicago. After living in Chicago for three years, the father left his family behind and rode the boxcars to Emerson and from there he reached h is sister's place. Here he took up a homestead on the Minnesota-Manitoba border.

Later he purchased a ¼ section of land just north of the original homestead under the survey registry of SW¼ Sect 22 Temp 1 Range 5E where he worked and lived till 1928 when he moved to the village of Tolstoi where he died August 19, 1930.

---

1 K. S. Prodan, THE LEADER, Winnipeg, 1931, p.35

Peter Kalushka

Peter Kalushka who came to Canada in 1911 from the village of Zboriw, married Hnat Galushka's youngest daughter Barbara. They moved to Lansing, Michigan where Peter worked in the Oldsmobile plant until 1921 when he returned to Tolstoi and bought an 80 acre farm. He raised livestock and poultry. He added another quarter section of land and continued with livestock. He bought a threshing outfit and did custom threshing. During the winter he bought grain. His son Myroslaw was born in Lansing.

The Kalushkas left Tolstoi to live in Winnipeg and in 1967 left for Windsor, Ontario where both died.*

The settlement around Tolstoi stretched from the Zolota school at Oleskiw's post office through Czervona S.D. (later Tolstoi) to the Bradley school district to the south.

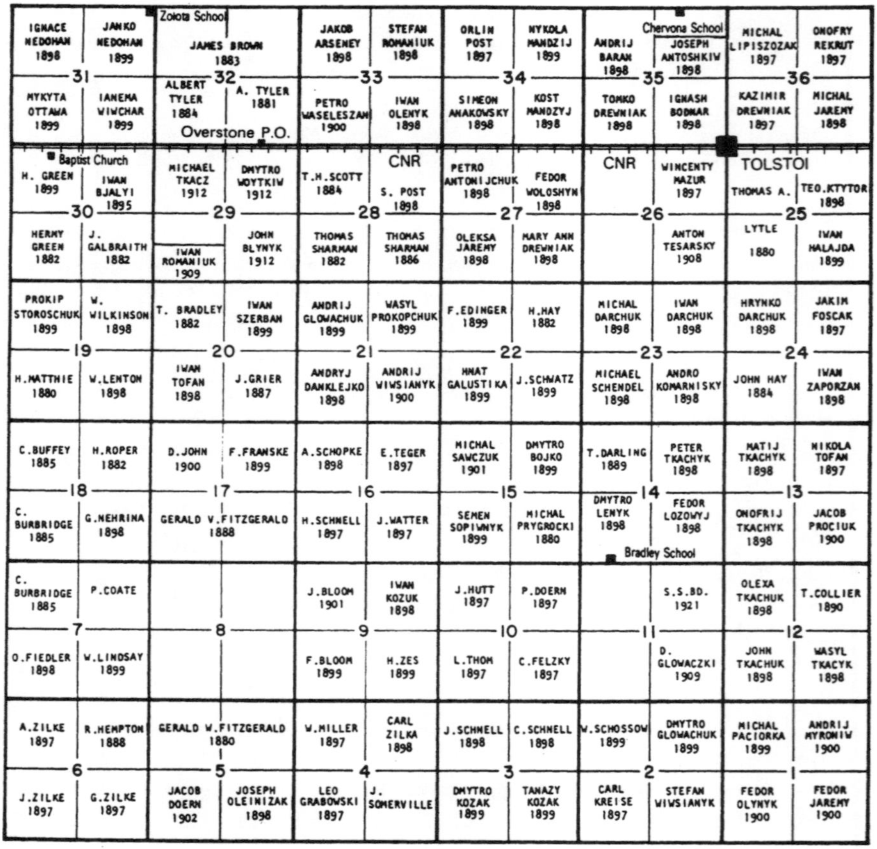

Fig. 3

---

* From information provided by Maurice Kalushka of Brandon in 1981.

Part III
Settlers Establish Firm Roots

Chapter 1

Civic Affairs

The Ukrainian settlers who took land to the east of the present hamlet of Stuartburn became interested in civic affairs from the start. The reason for this was that they did not receive much assistance from the municipality in which they settled in the organization of schools, development of roads and the draining of the land. Consequently, there was considerable dissatisfaction among the new farmers of the Stuartburn area. In 1900 a letter to the editor of the American Ukrainian newspaper Svoboda[1] by Michael Gudzmaniuk enumerates some of the sore points:

> Due to the fact that we do not know the English language and the ways of the country, due to a lack of leaders and a certain lack of cohesion among our people often we must swallow a bitter pill. Some officials, companies, traders (merchants), well-to-do English farmers, etc. often irritate the settlers and drive them to tears.
>
> In our colony such behaviour is part of a daily program, and more than anyone else the local merchant and at the same time the reeve of the municipality has annoyed us to the extreme. He "flays" the Ukrainians and cheats them, fools them, threatens them with legal action and takes advantage of them in every possible way: to one he sells land already claimed by other settlers; to the next he sells steamship tickets, and for the third he enters triple the amount of debt in the books. Often he makes trouble among the people in order that later, as reeve, he may make a settlement and, consequently, later it will be easier for him to take advantage of these men in some other way. The people are provoked by his actions and sore at him, but are unable to seek redress for they have not mastered the English language well enough!

Complaints were also made by the settlers about high taxes:

> Some were settled on such poor land that they have not even two morgens of cleared land, the rest is stone and sand...The taxes levied are equal to those of the English farmers, who may harvest a couple thousand bushels of grain....[2]

It appears that since the new settlers could not get any reasonable consideration or even investigation of their complaints from the council of the Rural Municipality of Franklin, they appealed to the Provincial government and in 1902 a new municipality of Stuartburn was created. The first councillors were: George Prygrocki, Peter Maykowski, S. Saranchuk and Ivan Machnie.

---

1 Svoboda, No. 34, 1900
2 Ibid, 11 April 1901

By the 1903 election the municipal council was changed somewhat and was made up of the following people: Ivan Probizansky, Wasyl Stefura, Nicholas Prygrocki and Samuel Tyron. Theodozy Wachna was the first secretary-treasurer and J. L. Ramsey was reeve.[3]

Theodozy Wachna in his reminiscences writes:

> ...It was difficult for us to achieve this, but we had a good community and the people worked well together. When the municipality was organized I was appointed secretary but this had difficult aspects also: the Municipal Commissioner did not want to accept my bond. Faced with problems of this type our settlers did not give up hope but worked as best they could. They well knew that Canada was their permanent home and will be the native land of their children. They strove to the maximum of their capacity to attain a better life. They needed schools, roads, bridges and other exigencies which the life of the day demanded.

The terms of settlement in the creation of the new municipality were rather harsh. The settlers, after paying taxes on their land for six years, were obliged to pay the municipality of Franklin a sum of $13,000 to be able to clear their lands of any further connections with the old organization.

Once the municipality was organized the municipal council soon realized that the municipality of Stuartburn could not bear the heavy costs of draining the land and needed the support of the Provincial government. The Rat and the Roseau rivers created problems. The Roseau River remained at a high water level for most of the year and was subject to flooding carrying the water of the drainage ditches draining the land of the Minnesota farmers. The MLAs, it seemed, were too absorbed in the development of the Emerson-Dominion City section of the constituency. The people decided that they needed a Member of the Legislative Assembly who would champion their cause.

* * * * *

Moving the Municipal Offices to Vita

With the municipal office of the new municipality in Stuartburn, the few Anglo-Saxons west of the hamlet continued to influence and direct the administration to a very marked degree. However, to the east Vita was attaining the status of the leading hamlet, consequently, the municipal office was moved to Vita and Joseph Kulachkowsky became secretary-treasurer, serving for two years. He was followed by Michael Kadyniuk, a Zhoda school teacher who, like Dmytro Yakimischak came from the Pleasant Home district near Teulon. Both received their preparation for teaching in Dr. Hunter's Boys' Home.

The moving of the Municipal Hall to Vita gave the hamlet more status.

---

3 M. Marunchak, "Studies in the History of Ukrainians in Canada". Vol. 11, Winnipeg 1966-67 p.42

From the start the hall was used as a cultural centre and concerts and plays were staged in it.

From its inception as a municipality, the R.M. of Stuartburn struggled with the lack of funds to make improvements in the area: to build the roads and to drain the swamps to make more land arable. To a degree there was political struggle and political turmoil. The almost annual change in reeves to administer the area appears to attest for this. In review the situation appeared as follows:

The first reeve of Ukrainian extraction to be elected in any municipality in Manitoba was Ivan Storosczuk.[4] He became reeve of the Rural Municipality of Stuartburn in 1908. The others to serve this municipality were: N. Hawryluk, 1911-12;

N. Gushulak, 1913-14; Nykola Eliuk, 1915-16; N. Bodnarchuk, 1922; Joseph Kulachlowsky, 1923-24, 1926; Anton Malliniuk, 1925; Theodozy Wachna, 1927.

Mr. Wachna who became the first secretary when the municipality was organized was the last reeve when it was disorganized in 1927. He was around to drive the last spike into the coffin of the organization he helped to create.

There is no doubt that had the area had an M.L.A. who was anxious to devote more effort; and had the Provincial governments been willing and had people with imagination to help develop an agricultural approach suitable to the area, it may have developed. True, the Department of Agriculture did make the services of its representative, K. S. Prodan, available and he provided good leadership, but there was a lack of financial assistance and a considerable degree of disenchantment.

C.(K) S. Prodan

4 Paul Yuzuk, The Ukrainians in Manitoba, University of Toronto Press, 1953, p.181

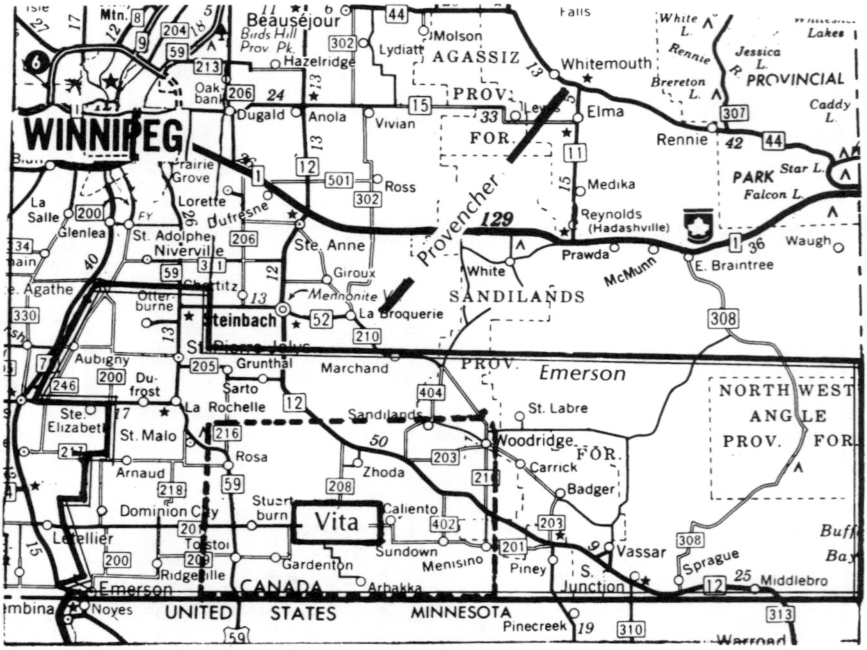

Fig. 4 Vita is the centre of the Ukrainian settlement found in the constituencies of Emerson and Provencher.

Chapter 2

Organization of Churches

During his visit Reverend Nestor Dmytriw's suggestion to the people that they needed a church and a Ukrainian Catholic clergyman was taken seriously. Before him, Dr. Joseph Oleskiw recommended to the government that land be set aside for a church and also a place where a residence could be built for a married clergyman with enough arable land so he would be able to support himself before the community was large enough to support a married clergyman.

St. Michael's Ukrainian Orthodox Church

The first Orthodox church parish was organized in 1897, but the building of the church did not commence. Unfortunately, a division erupted among the pioneers whether the church should be built on the east or west side of Roseau River. Those from the village of Bridok (Wasyl Zahara's village) lost in a vote and those from the village of Onut won. Consequently, the first Ukrainian Orthodox church in Manitoba was built on the southwest side of the river, on a land grant from the Federal Government and a pioneer cemetery was established on the church grounds. It was called the St. Michael's (Onut) church. Later the St. Demitrios Orthodox church was built east of Gardenton. (At the present time there is a fine Ukrainian Orthodox church in Gardenton)

Fig. 1 St. Michael's Ukrainian Greek Orthodox Church

Fig. 2 St. Demitrios Ukrainian Greek Orthodox Church. (Courtesy of Rev. John A. Melnyk)

The members of these churches were adherents of the Greek Orthodox faith; however, the majority of the settlers, northeast of the Roseau River were Ukrainian Catholics then called Greek Catholics who wanted their own Greek Catholic clergy. However, their efforts were frustrated by the Roman Catholic curia that informed the governmental officials that in the Red River and west they had the requisite clergy to minister to the Ukrainian Catholic settlers and there was no need to have clergy come form Western Ukraine (Halychyna).

In the meantime the coming of the Ukrainian Catholic missionary was arranged by Dr. Oleskiw. He was a married man, a distinguished composer, Reverend Ostap Nizankowsky. His coming, however, was cancelled; and Dr. Oleskiw's request for funds to help a clergyman get started was also declined by the Government; Dr. Oleskiw was informed that the Roman Catholic church was prepared to look after the spiritual welfare of his immigrants.[1]

Reverend Kulawy's Visit

As far as the Roman Catholic church was concerned, it was prepared to assist and Archbishop Langevine had a clergyman in readiness for missionary work among the Oleskiw settlers. He was Reverend Albert Kulawy, who was trained to serve the Polish people in the New Country. Archbishop Langevine also favoured small-holding patterns of settlement that were to start in St. Norbert and East Selkirk. As a consequence of Reverend Kulawy's visit, a Roman Catholic chapel was built in the Vita area and another one in Overstone which was later moved to Tolstoi.

The Church Dilemma

The members of St. Michael's church could not get a clergyman of their own either and had to depend on the clergy from the Russian Orthodox church in the USA. Since the Russians and the Poles were historical oppressors of the Ukrainian people, a very unhappy situation evolved and even split the Ukrainian Catholic group. They not only built a church in Stuartburn, they built two. One group did not want to accept Archbishop Langevine's tutelage. This situation led to discord and unhappiness in the settlement.

The Genik Solution

Cyril Genik who provided solid leadership during the land acquisition period, wanted to find a solution to the discord, and, therefore, through contact with Reverend Ahapius Honcharenko[2] in California, it was arranged for Bishop Seraphim to come to Canada to provide leadership in the formation of a church that would be neither under the Polish nor Russian influence. It was to be an Independent Orthodox church.

Independent Orthodoxy consequently even appealed to some Greek Catholics as two clergymen became available. One Hryhorij Prygrocki who was an ordained priest by Archbishop Seraphim, the other was Reverend N. Roshko. This church organization was not a success. And as Ukrainian Catholic clergy began to visit the settlements; it ceased to exist.

As more Greek Orthodox settlers came into the area, they established churches in Arbakka and even made an error and built one south of the bor-

---

1 V. J. Kaye, Early Ukrainian Settlements in Canada, pp. 69-70.
2 The first known Ukrainian to come to U.S.A. before 1880.

der. Their early clergy were laymen ordained by the Russian Orthodox church hierarchy in the USA; at least one, Reverend Evasiuk, was a resident farmer.

Vita Area

Though there was a Roman Catholic chapel, however, the Ukrainians built a church a mile and a quarter northwest of Vita. Eventually, a split developed and one group moved the church into the hamlet. It became a Ukrainian Orthodox church. The Ukrainian Catholics built a fine church about a half mile north of the hamlet and after 1920 both churches had resident clergy.

Tolstoi Churches

In Tolstoi, though the Roman Catholics moved a chapel into the hamlet, the Ukrainian Catholics built a church. Eventually, the influence of a school teacher Wasyl Kudryk (who later became editor of "Ukrainian Voice" – and still later was ordained clergyman of the Ukrainian Orthodox church) - who opposed the matter of transferring the church property to the Catholic Bishop's Corporation, nearly half of the parishioners organized the Ukrainian Orthodox Church.

Fig. 3 Ukrainian Catholic Church, Tolstoi

Fig. 4 Ukrainian Catholic Church, Stuartburn

West of Tolstoi, close to the site of Oleskiw Post Office, a Baptist church came into being. This small group did have a church, but did not associate much with the other two groups.

Rosa-Senkiw-Sarto

The settlement here was north of Stuartburn, but as far as organization of churches was concerned, the same pattern was followed. In spite of the proximity of the Ukrainian settlers in the Rosa-Sarto area to the French in St. Malo and the Mennonite churches to the east, no association developed.

Though relations between the two church groups on the start were acrimonious, at the present time, however, they are good and the two cooperate in local projects. This they did earlier when Reverend Peter Sametz, a certified teacher, was hired to teach at the junior level in the Shevchenko school.

Through the years, the members of the two churches had a keen appreciation and respect for their culture and traditions. Credit is due to both groups that they adhered to their ethnicity and the communist element never established a foothold in the areas as did happen in the Interlake region of Manitoba.

Church Parishes

Ukrainian Catholic

Church parishes where fine churches were erected may now be found in these destricts: Caliento, Lonesand, Rosa, Sandilands, Sopivnyky, Stuartburn, Sundown, Tolstoi, Vita and Zhoda.

Ukrainian Orthodox

Arbakka, Gardenton hamlet, St. Michael's, St. Dmitrios, Rosa, Sarto, Senkiw, Sirko, Tolstoi and Vita.

In recent years the Ukrainian Baptists have erected a small church at Roseau River and highway 59, no doubt, replacing the church that once operated at Overstone.

The area east of Dominion City and Emerson was fortunate that with a grant from a kind Pilot Mound, Manitoba woman a hospital was built by the United Church in Vita. Dr. H. Waldon of Killarney came to take charge.

In addition to the services provided for their congregations by the two main churches in the area, the staff of the Vital hospital also had a small chapel in the hamlet where Sunday school classes were held. The United Church, however, did not seem able to get established in the area or to gain many adherents.

Several families established residence in Emerson and a greater number in Pembina, N.D. At one time the Ukrainian Orthodox clergyman used to hold services in Pembina, N.D.*

Fig. 5 Ukrainian Catholic Church, Caliento

Fig. 6 Ukrainian Orthodox Church, Vita

As far as it is possible to ascertain, only one man from the area entered the Ukrainian Catholic priesthood, though on the start some boys received their education in St. Boniface. As far as the Orthodox group was concerned, following in the footsteps of the Very Reverend Wasyl Kudryk, three clergymen of the Ukrainian Orthodox church from the area, were ordained, Reverend Michael Shkrumeda, Reverend R. Bozyk from Vita and Reverend Nahirniak from the Sarto-Trentham district.

Cemeteries and Forsaken Cemeteries

In the new land in the Canadian west as the settlements were established the immediate demand was to set aside a parcel of land for a cemetery. Such was the onus placed on the Oleskiw settlers who came into the inhospitable land east of the Roseau River. They, therefore, established a cemetery along a trail between Stuartburn and another early community of Shevchenko, a mile north of the present hamlet of Vita.

This first cemetery was located in the middle of Section 22 with each homesteader donating a quarter of the space. This cemetery was in continuous use until a Ukrainian Catholic cemetery was organized three miles east of Stuartburn and now is well cared for. The first cemetery was abandoned. People moved away, fires burned down wooden crosses and now only a few stone markers erected later remain. Farmers fenced their "quarters" and it remains inaccessible now.

Before many years a new group known as the Bishop Seraphim or Independent Orthodox came into being and this group started a cemetery on Wasyl Saranchuk's farm. After a few years, this group lost its followers, and

* At the present time we have been informed only three Ukrainian families live in Pembina.

there was no one to take care of the plots. And now it seems that part of it has been ploughed.

Wasyl Zahara was the first one from south of the Dnister River to come with the Oleskiw group. Later as more of his kinfolk arrived from the Province of Bukovyna, and they established a cemetery and built the St. Michael's Orthodox Church. The cemetery beside the church - now declared a historical site - has received good care for a century.

In 1996, a century after the Oleskiw settlers arrived in the area east of Emerson, a Free Press reporter visited the area and reported on an abandoned cemetery:

> A visit to the cemetery…was..a sobering session on the hardships of life in a land that was never meant to be inhabited by struggling farmers. What are the reminders?
> …An old cedar cross, its arms broken and bent, stand guard over the graves of 36 Ukrainian settlers who struggled during life to survive in a harsh and uninhabitable land.

There was a school in the area, too, known as Border School, but it was moved to another site.

The St. Nicholas Orthodox Church in the area burned down and all that is left is the foundation.

Fig. 7 This cross was placed here by George Oprsk in 1918. Courtesy Winnipeg Free Press

According to the Free Press report, John Podolsky located the grave of his grandparents and so did George Demaniuk; and with the help of other people, cleared the cemetery and hammered in the ground in front of each grave a numbered marker.

John Podolsky sadly reminisced:

They didn't know what awaited them when they left the train station in Winnipeg (in 1896) to travel to their new homes…and when they got here most of them could not afford to turn back…

Fig. 8 The long-abandoned graveyard amidst its federal pasture land
Courtesy Winnipeg Free Press

And now they rest in this forsaken cemetery in the middle of a community pasture.

It appears that it is incumbent on the clergy now in the area to check on the abandoned resting places of pioneers and ensure that the cemeteries received proper care.

The Kawulia Tragedy

This cemetery gained notice when a tragedy befell a husband and wife and they are buried there. This was in the early thirties.

Some years bears from western Ontario and Minnesota often used to wander to the west, into the settlements. "One day during the haying season as we were getting ready to bring a load of hay from our prairie farm, our neighbor came running to us. He seemed very excited and gesticulated excitedly."

"Have you heard of the Kawulia tragedy?" he called to us from a distance.

"What tragedy?" asked my husband.

"They are both dead!"

It so happened that this summer the bears following the Roseau River came to the area around Gardenton. At noon one big fellow followed the cows to the farm yard and started to drink from the trough. Mr. Kawulia saw him and set the dogs on him. The bear ran away and climbed a tree nearby. So the old fellow and his boys took a shotgun and fired at him; but they only had one cartridge. (The beast wasn't bothering them so why did they have to get all excited?) Mr. Kawulia then went to the shed and came out with a scythe tied to a pole. As he poked at the beast, the bear bit at it and cut his mouth badly. He then grabbed the scythe and broke it in two, but he cut his paws. Then he started to come down.

The young fellows ran away, but Mr. Kawulia was going to attack the bear with a pitch fork. The bear lunged at him, and as Mr. Kawulia was backing away he tripped on a stone and fell. With one swipe of his paw, the bear disemboweled him. When Mrs. Kawulia saw the gore, she fell and died on the spot.

That evening when we came to the Kawalia home, they were laid out on a catafalque — like a bride and groom.

Now their resting place is an abandoned cemetery in Township 1 and Range 7 that is nestled deep in the heart of a swamp, rock-infested community pasture.

* * * * *

Many who left Canada for the U.S.A. did not forget their Canadian roots. One of them was a Gardenton-born John Panchuk who though an American citizen worked hard to have the St. Michael's church where he was baptized declared an historical site.*

* The St. Michael's church observed its centenary on the 14th of August 1997, with Metropolitan Wasylyj singing Mass on that occasion.

Chapter 3

Organization of Schools

While the Oleskiw settlers held homesteads in the R.M. of Franklin the only school that their children could attend was Stuartburn, and some did. It was too far for others to walk to that school and children were growing up without an opportunity to learn English. When the settlers requested that schools be built to the east of Stuartburn, they were counseled to build their own.

Nevertheless, those who attended the Stuartburn school showed good progress. This is verified by Inspector A. L. Young's report of 1897:

> Large number...who have lately settled on the vicinity of Stuartburn increased the school population...The children are bright, intelligent and most anxious to acquire knowledge of English language. They are well behaved in school and easily managed. (Their progress is very satisfactory)[1]

In addition to these observations Inspector A. L. Young also observed that there were many settlers in the Purple Bank school district (now Gardenton) that has been disbanded, and that he visited the area and suggested the ratepayers re-open the school.[2]

Then in 1901 Inspector A. L. Young again stressed the ability of the children from Ukrainian homes, and that they were acquiring the knowledge of English in a short time. He added that the new ratepayers attend a meetings and take an active interest in school matters to insure that their children get a good education.

However, when the Oleskiw settlers broke away from the R.M. of Franklin, and formed the R.M. of Stuartburn, there were no schools to the south-east of Stuartburn and the settlers began to organize districts in rapid succession. Records of the Department of Education show that the organization proceeded as follows

Though the oldest school in the area settled by Oleskiw settlers was Stuartburn, organized Oct. 10, 1888. It carried the number 556. Bradley school, however, carrying the number 369 preceded it. It was organized in 1880. Some Anglo-Saxon settlers also settled on the south side of the Roseau River where the hamlet of Gardenton is now located, and in 1891 a school named Purple Bank was organized even though the population appears to have decreased to the extent that the school was closed, but was re-organized with the coming of the Ukrainians.

The first school to be organized by the Ukrainians was named Lukowce. It was organized by Ukrainians who came from the province of Bukovyna, and consequently the third school district was named Bukovyna organized, 03 February 1903, the same time as by Koroliwka. The first school north-east of Stuartburn

1 Vidi, B. N. Bilash, Bilingual Public Schools in Manitoba 1897-1916, p.36
2 Ibid.

was Svoboda, later renamed Beckett. It was organized on the 4th of August 1903. Shevchenko school, now located in the village of Vita district came into being, 03 July 1906 and was preceded by Arbakka, organized, 02 February 1904.

The organization date suggest that after settling in 1896, those who went east as far as Vita did not have a school for their children for ten years.

The delaying tactics of the administration of the R.M. of Franklin did a great injustice to the children of the new settlers, and consequently the older children did not have an opportunity to attend school at all; when some schools came into operation, there were children seventeen years of age in grade one. Many received their early schooling in Ukrainian language at home.

Credit is due to the administration consisting mainly of Ukrainian settlers that the organization of schools in the new municipality commenced on

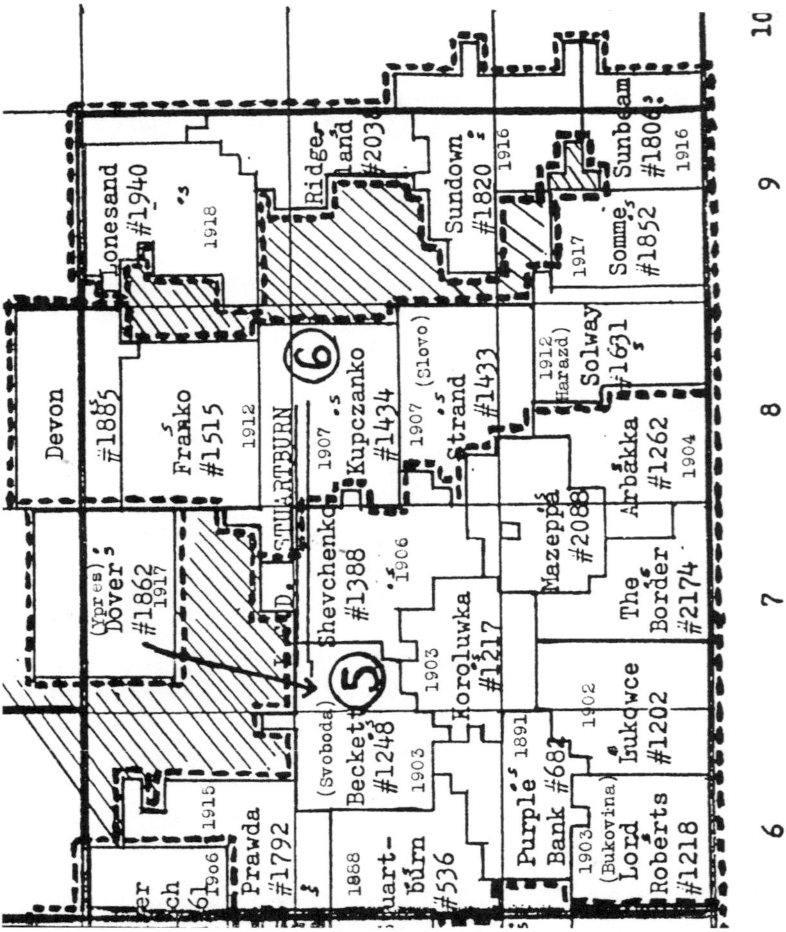

Fig. 1 Map showing the school districts location in the area.

the year of the formation of the municipality. The start was difficult for the municipality not only because it came into being without funds, but also because it was forced to pay the Rural Municipality of Franklin a sum or $13,000 severance pay. From the start the taxes in each school district went up to meet school debenture payments and teacher's salary.

Other districts were formed in time.

In 1903 when the R. P. Roblin government was formed a tolerable attitude to the bilingual school system was shown under the leadership of the Chief Clerk of Education Robert Fletcher. In the early years he appointed school organizers J. Baderski, Theo Styfanyk, T. D. Ferley and Paul Gigaychuk to help with the organization of schools among Ukrainian settlers.

Consequently, we note that due to the influence of local enlightened citizens and school organizers some schools were given Ukrainian names: Svoboda (Freedom), Beckett, Shevchenko (poet – Taras Shevchenko), Prawda (Truth), Bukovina (Lord Roberts), Lukowce, Czervona (Red), Zolota (Golden), Senkiw (name of village), Slovo (The Word), Harazd (All is Well) and Franko, Mazeppa, Morozenko, Kupchanko (Ukrainian historical names). Arbakka (the bank of a river) was an Icelandic name. Some Icelanders settled in the area earlier.

Bradley, Plankey Plains, Zolota, Czervona (later Tolstoi), Senkiw, Carlowerie, Baskerville and River Ranch remained in the Municipality of Franklin. Willow Plains and Sarto were in the R. M. of Hanover.*

Table I

List of Schools in R.M. of Stuartburn Showing Year of Organization

Stuartburn	10/1/88	Kupczanko	6/8/07
Bradley	17/6/85	Mazeppa	27/3/21
Purple Bank	13/10/91	Harazd (Solway)	4/6/12
Plankey Plains	12/6/00	Sunbeam	7/5/12
Lukowce	5/7/02	Slavna	7/5/12
Bukovyna (Lord Roberts)	3/2/03	Zelota	17/3/14
Koroliwka	3/2/03	Tolstoi	1914
Svoboda (Beckett	4/8/05	Carlowrie	12/9/14
Czervona	10/3/03	Prawda	3/6/15
Arbakka	2/2/04	Sundown	29/3/16
Senkiw (Rosa)	12/6/06	Baskerville	1/4/16
Shevchenko	3/7/06	Ypres (Dover)	8/3/17
River Ranch	13/3/06	Devon	25/5/17
Strand (Slovo)	6/8/07	Lonesand	2/7/18

* These schools later were phased into the School Division of Boundary.

Problem of Staffing Schools

When the first schools were organized, the Department of Education tried to staff them with permit teachers. Some were young girls with only a grade eight education. It was difficult for these people to get suitable accommodation – the homesteader's two-room house did not lend itself well to provide extra space for a teacher. In schools these young people did not have the requisite preparation to cope with the teaching of children who knew not a word of English, some were over age ranging from 7 to 17.

The Teaching Training Programme

The Conservative government of the day opened up a school in Winnipeg on Minto Street which was later transferred to Brandon. Graduates from these schools were specially trained to teach among their people. There was one positive feature about this: they were bilingual and used the Ukrainian language to help develop comprehension. In the Victoria readers the vocabulary was rather advanced.

There were young men in the area with a better education standing - some had started gymnasium. Those of the local men to take the course and return to teach were W. Saranchuk, B. W. Smuk, John and W. Kohut and Joseph Kulachkowsky. Their ranks were augmented by men from other areas.

Other early teachers were Geroge Machala, Theo Kochan, W. Mihaychuk and N. Kosowan, Mr. W. Kudryk who was from the Tolstoi area, a qualified teacher in the Ukraine, did teach in Bukovina district. Following these were Ostapovich, J. W. Jerowkski, Michael Kadyniuk, and one Mr. Salinos from Malta who married a local girl and taught in the area for many years, and so did Mr. Malyniuk.

The Young Teachers

Following in the footsteps of the teachers trained in the Minto school and the Training school in Brandon younger teachers with high school education received permits to teach. In the training a young group of men, Dr. Hunter's school in Teulon made an outstanding contribution.

The early teachers from the area who received their elementary and high school education were Peter Humeniuk, W. Nazarevich (from Tolstoi) and Miss Kolisnyk from Vita.

The work of Dr. Robert Fletcher of the Department of Education helped to provide teachers for rural areas. He interviewed capable people and gave them special permits to teach. Most of them carried and their assignments with commendable success. We shall centre our attention on a small group around the district knows as Rosa, MB. Some of them had to overcome many difficulties like Mr. Goresky did.

The Baskerville Teacher*

Mr. Isidore Goresky, grew up in Stonewall, received his high school education in Winnipeg and received a permit to teach in Tarno school north-east of Arborg. At the end of the first term he discontinued work there and was given a permit to teach in Baskerville school in the Rosa district.

From his memoirs we learn about the first-day difficulties he encountered, but eventually became a successful teacher and taught in the area for several years and at the same time took extra-mural university courses.

Going to Baskerville School

The train journey did not present any difficulty. Trains were scheduled to reach Arnaud between six and seven o'clock in the evening. As Baskerville school was about twelve miles east, I had to spend the night with a family by the name of Jones who provided overnight accommodation for those who travelled by train. Both the families, Bundys (at Tarno) and Jones, have stuck in my memory: the man, in each case, was very small in stature in comparison to his wife; both the wives were tall women. As there was plenty of snow, I set out next morning with a man driving a horse and cutter. Coming out of that River Valley proper about six miles east, we stopped at a farmer's place, his name was Devott, to enquire about the rest of the road. Here a savage dog tore a mouthful of cloth out of my overcoat. It was an embarrassment to meet new people with a torn coat, more so for as I got out of the cutter at my new boarding place I tore my suit on a nail.

I was to board with the Paul Koroluk family but they left to the Ostafijiws who lived about three-quarters of a mile east. There that night most of the community had been invited as it was some sort of holiday. In my memory the holiday appeared to be Christmas day according to the Julian calendar, but the fact that there was a dance night, it could have been New Year's day.

Later I discovered that my arrival was not as inconspicuous as it had appeared to me. There were comments about my torn clothes and also about my Ukrainian language. It was understandably weak, but the weakness was attributed to the fact that I spoke with a Bukowinian accent. I was, however, very happy that I had reached this destination and found the community attractive from the beginning.

It was during that first spring I acquired a bicycle with which I could visit two local teacher friends, Peter Humeniuk in River Ranch school and Peter Roscoe in Senkiw. The road to Peter Humeniuk's was always open though it went through farmers' yards. He boarded at Pupezas about a half mile east of where the community hall was built. As the three of us had bicycles, we travelled on Sundays to what was known as Mosquito Creek, near St. Malo, where Peter Roscoe's brother farmed. There were three girls in the family and they usually had visitors from many areas.

(All three teachers married local girls, but only Isidore Goresky completed university and attained a post-graduate degree.)

In the neighboring settlement of Sarto, a teacher Mr. John Nykyforuk gave good leadership in the community. According to Mr. Goresky, he had a

* From Isidore Goresky, Reminiscences: Materials provided for the author.

good library. At that time John Boitsun taught in Willow Plains and Sarto.

These younger teachers served as an inspiration to the young people in the district to go into teaching. From the Peter Tanchak home in Rosa five became teachers.

In the early twenties one factor that kept teachers in rural areas was that on the average they received $95 a month, and a free teacherage and fuel.

During the late twenties and early thirties there were over a hundred young men and women from the area who became teachers.

Also three men went into professions. Elias Wachna and Manolyj Mihaychuk became dentists. Theodore Ewanchuk became a doctor, but died before he could commence practice. Later Alec Danylchuk of Sandilands graduated as a doctor.

It is notable, however, that during this period, there were few women from the Ukrainian settlers' homes to be engaged as teachers. One of the early women teachers was Mary Koreska from Winnipeg. She had a successful year in Lukowce school.

From the Sandilands area Peter Olchoweski became a successful high school teacher and his brother Alexander got his PhD, and was a professor at the University of Manitoba.

Mr. S. Drul went to be a lawyer in Saskatchewan. O. Lukianchuk left for Alberta.

Mr. John Eliuk was born in Arbakka, got his degree, saw military service and taught in Shevchenko school. Mr. Bob Cysmestruk is serving as the principal of Shevchenko Collegiate. John Machyla completed Grade XII and took over his father's farm.

Getting an elementary education for children who grew up on backwoods and swampy homesteads was not an easy matter. In the first place lack of roads impeded regular attendance. In western Canada during the early years there was a shortage of teachers in all areas, the situation was more acute in the less accessible parts of the province, and such was the case in the newly formed municipality of Stuartburn. Children had to help with the meager

Fig. 2 Country children on their way to school.

harvests and attendance during September was low. Parents, however, encouraged their children to study and to attend school. "Get an education, and you will not have to toil and struggle as hard as we do."

It was not uncommon for mothers to help their children by going with them part way to school. In the Senkiw area, for instance, one family was cut away from school by a creek. When the water was high, the mother, in this case, would go with her children, hitch up her skirt and carry them one by one across the creek. Then she had to meet them in the afternoon to make it possible for them to come home.

To start with the people found the bilingual system of education a boon. Older children went to work and needed to be able to write home in Ukrainian so that the parents would understand. They learned the basics of both languages in school after teachers who could teach both languages were available.

End of Bilingualism

After the defeat of the R.P. Roblin's government, T.C. Norris became Premier and his first "great" act was to abolish the bilingual system of education. And it is claimed that he ordered the bilingual readers – Ukrainian and others – burned on the Legislative grounds. After that one teacher, it is said, drew a picture with T. C. Norris, pitch fork in hand – emulating Satan - kept stoking the fire with readers, and the civil servants hurling flaming copies into the darkness. It really was a horrific act, damnable may be a better word.

Fig. 3 Rural School

Fig. 5 Children and teacher of Kupchanko School in the Vita School Field Day.

Fig. 6

Chapter 4

The Rosa Group*

Maria Paley (nee Maksymchuk)

Maria Paley was born in the village of Laniwtsi to Oleksa and Wasylyna Maksymchuk on 14 October 1882. Maria's father with wife and child left his ancestral village of Bilche Zolote to work as a forester in Laniwtsi. Shortly thereafter, Maria was born. Her parents later moved back to Bilche Zolote at the urging of Oleksa's father, Tanasiya. Leaving for Canada after father died, Oleksa's right to inherit his father's property was contested by one of his brothers. Consequently, they decided to emigrate to Canada, as they were impressed by the accounts received from a close friend, Kost Nemirsky, and a relative, Kost Manziy, of life in the Stuartburn settlement of southern Manitoba. Oleksa sold his land for $500 and the entire family set off for Canada. Upon their arrival in the Stuartburn settlement on Ascension Day in the spring of 1901, Oleksa Maksymchuk immediately set out on foot for the Manziy farm, returning with Kost Manziy on a wagon drawn by what appeared to be a yoke of giant oxen.

Settled on Homestead

Maria's parents obtained a homestead six miles north of Stuartburn and though much of the soil on the farm was stony and a large portion consisted of muskeg; the entire family moved on to the homestead except Maria, who went to work as a housekeeper for the family of a grain elevator operator in Emerson. Having earned $18 in wages by the year-end, she returned to the family farm. Together with what her father had earned from working as a harvester, and the money earned by her mother, brother and sister from the sale of Seneca roots, they were able to buy lumber, a stove and flour. They had already purchased a cow and a calf from their remaining savings, and felt very fortunate.

Met Semen Paley in 1902

During the Christmas celebrations in January 1902, Maria met Semen Paley who in 1900 had emigrated with his father from the village of Senkiw. His mother, Oksana, had perished tragically in a fire in their home in Senkiw; subsequently, Oleksa brought his entire family of five children - Todyr, Semen, Wasylyna, Anne and Ivan - to Canada, settling in Senkiw.

Semen and Maria were married by a Polish priest at the end of the Christmas season, on St. John the Baptist's Day (the Feast of Jordan - January, 19). As neither of the betrothed understood Polish, the wedding service had to be translated to them by a fellow Ukrainian and their wedding reception followed twelve days later.

---

* Based on Isidore Goresky memoirs.

The newly-married couple lived with Semen's father and his family for a short time before moving to a small house on Wasyl Tanchak's land in the Senkiw area. Semen, while searching for Seneca roots, found 240 acres of good land for sale, at a price of $1000. It was located about four miles northeast of Senkiw. Having put a down payment of $140 on this land in 1904, Semen and his younger brother Ivan (John) built a small hut which served as a temporary residence for the family. A larger house in the traditional Ukrainian style was constructed from tamarack logs and completed in 1908.

In the new house, Semen and Maria raised their family: Anne, Wasyl, Nicolas, Peter and Zonia. In the Paley house Greek Catholic priests were accommodated. It also served as a place of worship where couples were married and children baptized. It served as a meeting place for local community organizations: a library was kept there until the Ukrainian Narodnyj Dim was built in 1919.

John Paley built a new house for his family by the road allowance to the east of the property in 1918. It was constructed in a more modern style and was considerably larger than the traditional two-room style of Semen's house. The church was built in 1923 and they served on the executive of parish committees: Maria as the head of the church sisterhood and Semen as head of the church committee. During this period, Semen also took over responsibility for the store, located in a building on his property, which his brother had previously operated out of his own house.

River Ranch School

The River Ranch school was the first school in the Rosa district. Then the Baskerville school was constructed in 1918 and the children attended it until moving to Winnipeg to continue their high school education.

When Semen's health began to fail in 1941, he divided his land among his sons. Semen and Maria subsequently moved to Winnipeg, where they remained until Semen's death in 1946. Following his death, Maria moved to Edmonton to live with her daughter Zonia to be closer to her daughter, Anne, Mrs. Isidore Goresky and son, Wasyl, who also lived in Alberta.

In 1976 as she began to lose her sight and hearing, she was admitted to a nursing home where she died in March 1978. She was buried beside her husband at Rosa, Manitoba.*

Lawrenty Dzyniak

I am a late comer. I came to Dominion City in 1929, so you can't class me as a real pioneer. During the First World War I served in the Russian army. Then I was in the Ukrainian army of liberation and was wounded three times

*Information provided by Mr. Isidore Goresky of Surrey, B.C.

during battles in Odessa. We were not able to remain independent and I experienced the Communist regime in my native "Chomska Gubernia".

When we arrived here, I rented a farm for a year and then moved to the Arnaud district where I bought a quarter section for taxes. I paid $4.00 an acre for it. Since we did not have much money left, I went to work for a farmer at $6.00 a month and used to come home in the evening, clearing land late into the night. My wife took care of and worked the farm while I was away and we got along. Then we bought the second quarter, paying $30.00 an acre.

There were very few Ukrainians here from the Greater Ukraine; they were mostly from the province of Western Ukraine and Bukovyna. We were Orthodox and joined the Ukrainian Orthodox congregation at Rosa. This helped us become part of the community, as earlier we were classed as Russians.

I got to know Mr. Harry Bugera who was a successful farmer in Dufrost. He gave me good advice about buying land and machinery.

We did not experience much happiness in life; it was a continuous struggle to make ends meet. Cost of machinery was very high; but life was better than under Stalin. When I think about the millions that were exterminated I can hardly credit it. If any person just tried to express himself too freely, he was taken away - no tears and pleadings by the wife and children were heeded. The man was shot.

Our only daughter, Mary, was our greatest source of joy. She is a school teacher here and her husband Tymko Chubey runs our farm. My wife died five years ago. I have a bad hip - it has been troubling me for fifteen years. Besides this I have had to have eye surgery and now I cannot read - I need someone to read to me. But I am pleased with life here: They certainly take good care of us. Life is good in this Vita Personal Care Home.

I would say that I have been a good Canadian and am being repaid kindly for this. I got along well with my neighbors; who, in the majority, were Mennonites and French. The Mennonites are clannish. They stick together and always consider you as an outsider. The French, on the other hand, have shown us more warmth: They have been easier to live with and they gave you a chance.

I am 82 years old and my productive years are behind me.

Theodore (Todosiy) Maksymchuk

I, Todosiy Maksymchuk, was born on May 2, in the village of Bilche Zolote, district of Borshchiw, Halychyna, to Oleksa and Wasylena (nee Olynyk) Maksymchuk residents of the same village. Oleksa was also a mail carrier. I went to school for two years and studied both Ukrainian and Polish. The family arrived in Canada on May 2, 1901, and first went to live with relatives from the same village, the Mandziys in Tolstoi. From there Oleksa filed for a quarter NE12-3-R5E of the First Meridian about six miles northeast of Stuartburn. I lived with my parents but was unable to attend school as the closest school at that time was Plankey Plain. Toward the end of 1909 or beginning of 1910 my sister Kalyna married Paul Koroluk. They lived with my parents for a year and their son Michael was born here. In 1910 I and Paul, having a hundred dollars each as a down payment, bought two hundred acres partly on SE33 and partly on SW34.

As to the early settlers the two Carleton brothers were in Rosa before anyone else. The Chubeys resided on section 11 near the Roseau River and did not move to the Rosa area until after first Bugera and later the Paleys had settled there.

I married Maria Bzovey on June 5, 1913. She had been born on December 17, 1896, in the village of Senkiw to Andrew and Hafia Bzovey of that village who had come to Canada about 1908. We lived with the Koroluks for a year and then moved across the road to a house they had built there. We lived in this house until 1920 when we bought 2 1/2 quarters from Tom Carleton across the Rat River. It was here that most of our family grew up and the children attended River Ranch school.

Other Settlers

As to other settlers in Rosa, John Pupeza married Maria's sister in Senkiw and came to Rosa about 1911. Peter Tanchak moved to his farm in Rosa a year after the Paleys had moved but Skrynski did not arrive in Rosa until after the First War.

Todosiy and Maria's children were as follows:

Wasyl married Helen Makowesky and lives in Toronto;
Dmytro married Nadia Mysak and lives in Hanover;
Ivan married Anne Gavronsky and was lost in the war;
Oleksa married Maria Kassian and lives in Winnipeg;
Natalia married Wasyl Romaniuk and lives in Roseau River;
Myroslaw is single and lives in Toronto;
Helen married Stefan Kruk and lives in Souris - NE13-7-21 and
Taras is also married and lives in Toronto.

My first wife died in 1964 and I married Anna (Farynyk) Smook who was widowed. She was the daughter of Ivan and Maria (Yawdoshyn) Farynyk. She was married in Senkiw in Halychyna in 1922 but came to Canada with her husband in 1924 to live in Rosa. My second wife lived on the farm until 1968 and then we moved to a new home we started in a new hamlet site which was named Roseau River as it is situated on the bank of this stream.

Nazarko Chubey

Nazarko Chubey was born on February 28, 1893, to Mykyta and Kateryna (Nykolayishen) Chubey in the village of Ivanie Puste, county of

Borshchiw, Halychyna, then Austria and now Ukraine. The family arrived in Canada in 1897 to settle in the Stuartburn area. When they came to Rosa in 1908, they bought land along the Rat River from a man named Charette. His father Mykyta bought it in partnership with his brother Tymko. They did not come alone at the time for two Olynyks came with them. Onufrey Olynyk was from the village of Bilche Zolote.

When they came to Rosa the two Carletons were already there. Holodryga arrived in Rosa about 1916 and Kassian settled about 1918.

Nazarko married Kateryna Diduch on November 9, 1914. She was the daughter of Kost and Maria Diduch who had also arrived from the village of Bilche Zolote. Kateryna died on October 2, 1975.

The Rosa District
Anton and Katyryna Mihaychuk (nee Danylchuk)

I, Anton Mihaychuk, was born January 01, 1895 in the village of Zazulyntsi in the district of Zalischyky in Western Ukraine. My parents were Semen and Anna (from the Mamalyga home). My father Semen was the son of Peter and my mother's maiden name was Tofan. She came from the neighboring village of Senkiw. On my mother's side, her parents were Maksym Mamalyga and Sofia Wiwchar.

My father used to tell us that two of his brothers lived across the river Dnister in the province of Bukovyna in the village of Bridok. Andrew and Peter were in Zazulyntsi.

We lived in the village and I attended school in the hamlet and completed grade three. Besides attending school I helped with farm work and also helped my married sisters.

I was seventeen years old when I came to Canada in 1912. I came along with Wasyl Ivonchuk's wife who was from the Ilnytsky home and was related to my mother. The Ilnytskys bought land to the east of Oleksa Maksymchuk. In the meantime Mr. Maksymchuk moved to a new farm which he bought from Peter Tanchak. This was in 1913.

Anton Mihaychuk recorded further as follows:

The first settlers at Rosa were the Carlton brothers...The first Ukrainian to buy land in the district was H. Bugera and then Palij who came from the Senkiw. After them came Chubey then Tanchak and later Ostafijiv, Pupyza, Mihay, Tofan and Onufrey Olynyk. And Skrynsky bought H. Bugera's farm. Bugera moved to Dufrost.
To start with Anton got employment with Carlton's herding cattle at $1.25 a head. He also herded for Theodocy Maksymchuk. Later he went further away to work for farmers and after working for one for four years, he saved enough money to be able to buy Panchyshyn's land. This was the farm where Theodocy Maksymchuk once lived. It was south of Baskerville school; Theodocy bought land from one of the Carltons on the other side of Rat River.

On January 01, 1922, Anton married Katyryna Danlylchuk, the daughter of Iwan and Paraska. Her mother's maiden name was Yakivets. The Yakivets family came to Canada from the village of Michaljkiv in the district of Borschiv, and settled in Gonor, MB. Then leaving their acres (not far from Winnipeg), they bought a farm in Arnaud in 1920, and later moved again to a farm in the district known as Mosquito Creek south of St. Malo.

Anton and Katyryna lived on their farm close to 50 years, and there their children attended Baskerville school. Their eldest daughter, Mary married Stefan Polischuk. they finally moved to Winnipeg. Peter married Jennie Kohut and they still live on their farm in Rosa. Wasyl married Katerina Manchulenko and they live in Winnipeg, too.

Anton and Katyryna left their farm and moved to Winnipeg; however, after a short try, they returned to Rosa where they rented a house built by Iwan Palij - just across the road from the church. They have seven grandchildren and fifteen great grandchildren.*

Iwan Kolodrubski		Ferdinand L'Heureux	Donald Fraser	Dmytro Andrushko	Andrij Bodnarchuk						
31		32		33		34		35		36	
Iwan Firymr	James W. Yeo	Ferdinand L'Heureux	Donald Fraser		Tekla Herman						
Petro Strumbicki		Harris L. Emmert	Alexa Korczak	Donald Fraser	Michal Herman	Wasyl Podelski	Wasyl Fesczuk	Hudson's Bay Company	Stanley Belinsky		John Kolsenyk
30		29		28		27		26		25	
Sawka Perun	Nykola Smuk	Harris L. Emmert	Harris L. Emmert	Larry S. Smook	Iwan Korczak	Iwan Podolsky	Mathij Podolski	Hudson's Bay Company	Hudson's Bay Company	Wladyslaw Belinski	John Kolisnyk
Kost Diduch	Iwan Iwonczyk	Wasyl Hawryluk	John Prokopchuk	Iwan Iwanicke	Wasyl Fochak	Joseph Kulaczkowski	Shmir & Bodnarczuk	Semen Kolisnyk	Maria Krawec	William Colquhoun	Stefan Danyluk / Thomas Sobistiansky
19		20		21		22		23		24	
Iwan Andrijiw	Ozarko Newransky	Nykola Cychmystruk	Michael Belinski	Petro Halasis	Onofrey Chornyj	Lena Kulachkowski	James W. Yeo	George Maczula	William Moroziuk / John Dymczuk	Stefan W. Fostey	
Hnat Iwonczyk	Hafija Michaniuk	John Wolf	Nykola Pachnowski	Province of Manitoba	Province of Manitoba	Michael Baczysnki	Wasyl Drul	Iwan Podolski	Phylyp Podolski	Joseph Dobranski	Anastasja Tymczuk
18		17		16		15		14		13	
Iwan Zahara	James Drew	Karol Wolf	Thomas Wolf	Province of Manitoba	Province of Manitoba	Nykola Baczysnki	Paulo Fedorowich	Stefan Krawec	Hrynko Podolski	Roman Lysak	Hawrylo Timchuk
John Baraniecki	Stefan Mokanuk	Hudson's Bay Company	Hudson's Bay Company	Antoch Yotcyshyn		James W. Yeo	James W. Yeo	School Land	School Land	Edward Dolynchuk	
7		8		9		10		11		12	
Dmytro Bugera		Hudson's Bay Company	Hudson's Bay Company	Demko Tkach	Anton Rymar	Louis F. Tollinger	Louis F. Tollinger	School Land	School Land		
Gawrylo Storozszuk	Michael Arsenie										
6		5		4		3		2		1	
Petro Kosteniuk	John Watling										

Fig. 1 Township 2, Range 7E.

*Translated from information provided in Ukrainian to Mr. Isidore Goresky and attached to a letter written September 01, 1977.

Chapter 5

Anglo-Saxon – Ukrainian Relationship

The sector of south-eastern Manitoba under study was settled, after 1885, by participants of the Saskatchewan Rebellion mainly; before the Ukrainians arrived in 1896, they had had there for ten years. Their attitude to the Metis and the French, understandably, was antagonistic.

When the first Ukrainian settlement was formed most of the Anglo-Saxons were pleased to be able to earn some money transporting goods for them by being able to sell cows, hogs and poultry as well as grain and vegetable seeds to start them on their homesteads - relationships were amicable, but not neighborly.

Nevertheless due to some petty fleecing, a rift developed. The new settlers dressed in their peasant garb tried to guard off fleecing by posing as being poverty stricken. But were they?

Here are some of the assessments about the financial resources of the Sifton settlers as they were soon to be called:

> ...they do not look s though they possessed any means, but each family claimed to have a considerable sum, the lowest being $70 and the highest, $400.
>
> (G. H. Mitchell 434026 General Register)

In Oct. 15, 1899:

> Twelve...families, sixty-eight persons carrying four thousand dollars left for the west by regular train.

Sept. 16, 1897:

> Ten families and eight single men (49 persons) carried $2200.

Sept. 19, 1897:

> 13 families and 6 single men declared $1564.

In time the situation changed.

Leaving Ukraine with more money than was required to pay for the transportation was difficult. Cyril Genik reported (1903-04) that immigration depreciated land values and land was hard to sell. However, in spite of this, once they arrived in Canada, they soon earned money, and repaid what they had borrowed to pay for transportation.

Reactions

It soon became evident in the west that the antagonism towards the new settlers was fanned by people in Eastern Canada, and by the members of some church groups. All early immigrants, though, were placed in the same boat. Here is an example of a churlish attitude:

> What's to be done with all these people – Icelanders, Swedes, Norwegians, Ger-

mans, Belgians, Austrians, Hungarians and others...[1]

In the June 2, 1899 issue, the Ottawa Free Press called the "new immigrants" dirty beasts".

Also in June 21, 1899 the Methodists at a conference assembled in Edmonton, deplored the immigration of Ukrainians.

And closer to the south-eastern rectangle of Manitoba, the editor of the Morden Chronicle responded expressing support for the attitudes of Eastern Canadians:

...though fairly good reports of progress have been made by visitors to the settlements of these people the fact, nonetheless, remains that (they) are not approved settlers.[2]

and then continued:

(Now)...that the steamship bonus...is about to be abolished, which practically means that that particular immigration will largely cease.[3]

The Chronicle concluded:

...The doubt in regards to (Ukrainians) is the fact that they have no kinship with us in blood.[4]

The Winnipeg Free Press defended the new immigrants and disagreed with claims, for instance, that Icelanders were undesirable, or that the Ukrainians were "neither useful nor ornamental". (In time there was an Icelandic settlement at Arbakka and south of Morden)

The Morden people and the farmers in the prairies soon found out that the Ukrainians were useful as workers and helped the farmer to bring in the bountiful harvests what led to the western Canada's agricultural success.

As far as blood relationship was concerned the Teutonic strain, no doubt, some of the Morden settlers did live long enough to see their sons and grandsons and the Ukrainians too, lay down their lives in wars to stem out the "pure-blood strain" attitude of European fanatics.

Nevertheless, it is necessary to stress again that the Morden Chronicle report appeared after a poem was published in the Saturday Night which seemed to set the tone for the attitudes among some people in the West.

Here is the racist diatribe in full:

Civilization is the white man's burden – a burden he is always ready to impose on the unfortunate barbarians who are still irresponsible and, frequently, happy. Is

1 The Progress, Preston, ON, May 26, 1899.
2 The Morden Chronicle, Morden, Thursday, May 25, 1899.
3 Ibid
4 Ibid

civilization a failure? Imagine my surprise, *fratres conscripti*, when Clark confronted me with that chestnut! Civilization a failure! Why demme, it's absurd so long as this catholic spirit pervades our Immigration Department! Listen:

Come in! Come in,
You frowsy Finn,
Likewise you Doukhobor!
Here is your goal,
You greasy Pole –
O, do not wander more!

Come too! Come too,
You Russian Jew
With dermal parasites!
Come right along
And join the throng
With other murky whites!

Come starch and stink,
You pasty Chink!
You nigerous and brown,
All hues, all creeds.
All smells, all breeds,
Come in and settle down.

No need to wash
And all that bosh,
Be ignorant as goats!
But on your necks
We'll brand our "X",
And see that you have votes!*

Consequently, due to the attitudes nurtured by the older settlers it took years before any "rapprochement" developed.

However, time, economic conditions and intermarriages did finally obliterate socially harmful attitudes and led to better social togetherness. Canadianism became stronger. Sir Clifford Sifton and Prof. Joseph Oleskiw helped to build the base for this great country, Canada.

---

* Vidi's Saturday Night, April 15, 1899.

Fig. 2 Young Ukrainian couple and child arriving in Canada. (Come in! Come in!)
(Courtesy Dr. V. J. Kaye and D. Hryhorovich)

Part IV
Making Progress

Chapter 1

The First Generation

The progress of the first Ukrainian settlement east of the Red River can best be put into prospective by giving a brief outline of the vertical development of a few men and women; by showing the efforts they had to make to succeed. This small sample will show that the Oleskiw settlers were a success in spite of the difficulties they had to face. Yes, it was Dr. Joseph Oleskiw who opened the gates for the Ukrainian settlers to come to the prairies of Canada. Nevertheless, it was the foresight, organizational ability and the programme of selecting the settlers by Clifford Sifton that led to the success of his immigration programme. He had a team of immigration officers who selected people with healthy bodies, willing and skilful hands and a good mental capacity. These people came to the Canadian prairies and stayed; they and their children and grandchildren made a fine contribution to make Canada a great country.

Peter Humeniuk - The Gentleman

Of those who were brought into the Stuartburn community as children, or were born during the early period of the settlement, Peter Humeniuk must be rated as a gentleman possessed with outstanding qualities of leadership. He got his elementary education in Stuartburn, attended Dominion City high school and completed his high school education while in residence in the Boys Home in Teulon. The programme there was organized by Dr. Hunter for the Presbyterian Church that did much to start many capable children from Ukrainian homes to better their own lot and then they, in turn, helped others to attain an education.

Mr. Humeniuk's desire to get an education was not an easy one. He happened to be the first boy from the home of a Ukrainian pioneer to attend the Stuartburn school located on the Roseau River where an early post office was located.

His first year in the Stuartburn school was a horrendous experience, very likely lived through by others, and very much a parallel to William Kurelek's experience in the Stonewall area.[1]

Now we report from what he personally recorded:[2]

> In November, 1906 I started school...I could read and write in Ukrainian and Polish but knew not a word of English...The additional problem was that out of an enrolment of 30 children, a six-year old girl, Mary Anne Wachna and I were the only ones of Ukrainian extraction...Amongst them there were several older boys who

---

1 M. Ewanchuk, William Kurelek: The Suffering Genius, Derksen Printers, Steinbach, MB, 1997.

2 As a close friend and mentor Mr. Humeniuk provided certain information and granted permission to use it and to quote from his book. (Ed.)
Peter Humeniuk, Hardships and Progress of Ukrainian Pioneers

greeted me and treated me like a savage...From the first day they made use of the recesses and the noon hour to maltreat me. Often when the teacher was not in the classroom during the noon recess, two or three of the older boys would grab me and hold my arms while one other would push snow behind my shirt collar. I was unable to defend myself physically or with words.

One very cold January day when the children were going home one boy jumped me and grabbed my cap (a homemade one) and I had to go home bareheaded and with my ears uncovered. Fortunately that day there was an older Ukrainian girl. Josephine Stephanowich saw me going along the road in tears and hatless so she gave me her large woolen shawl and she walked home bareheaded. I hope that the good Lord grants her many good years.

That's the way we were treated by ignorant people and their children followed their example.

When after several other maltreatments, one being hit in the eye with a snowball, my father complained to the trustees, and he contacted the teacher. I was punished the next day for being a "tattle-tale".

Being the oldest in the family, Peter Humeniuk was called upon to do work on the farm that he was too young to carry out. He related a story that when his father broke some new land, he was called upon to do the work with oxen while father was pulling roots and picking stones: He had to drive three oxen in the disc-harrow and they were not fully trained. At the end of the first day he showed his hands to his Mother. Since he had to guide the beasts with rope lines, he found out that the rope cut his hands horribly. Yet come the next day he was back at work.

In 1910 the district experienced a very dry year. There were forest and bush fires across the border in Minnesota. The forest in the Sandilands Reserve were also on fire. The animals, to escape the fire, followed the rivers and black bears were seen to come as far west as Gardenton and Tolstoi. Children were afraid to go into the bush, yet cows had to be brought home for milking.

The C.N.R. Railways Goes East from Emerson to Sprague

The extension of the railway line to the east of Emerson put an abrupt stop of Dominion City being the shopping centre for the settlement. Mr. Humeniuk made this observation:

About 1910 the Canadian National Railway extended its line, that connected Ridgeville with Emerson, to run farther east passing through Ukrainian settlements and thus creating new stations: Tolstoi, Gardenton, Vita, Caliento, Sundown...were joined by the rail line with South Junction. This railway line improved communication facilities for the settlers but was not a profit making line for the C.N.R.

Though there were few roads developed in the Stuartburn area, yet a bridge was built across the Roseau River at Stuartburn. It, no doubt, was a political project. Peter Humeniuk had an experience with the new bridge he never forgot: He recorded that at Stuartburn on the Roseau River:

> The bridge was about 150 feet wide, therefore, "to strengthen the wooden bridge which spanned the river, three quarter inch steel bars were secured close to each other under the planks." Several of us young boys were under the bridge one day (in 1907) and for some unknown reason I boasted that by grabbing each of these steel bars I would be able to cross the river by going under the bridge.

He continued:

> I carried out my undertaking but never again in my life did I experience such fear as I did on reaching the midpoint when I began to feel that my arms lacked the strength to grasp another bar. I felt that my arms would not last to carry me to the end. But when I looked at the river below where the water was deep and ran swiftly, I was overtaken with fear and this gave me the necessary strength to reach the other side of the river bank.

Six Years in Stuartburn School

In my six short years of schooling in the Stuartburn school we had several English speaking teachers. Of them and the most capable one was an elderly, grey-haired teacher, Mr. Barrell. He used to teach the children very wisely and was most devoted to his task. It was likely due to his advanced age that he developed a habit of dozing off at his desk at precisely fifteen minutes before twelve noon.

As a result of the respect the children had of his age they behaved quietly during his nap and continued with their lessons.

And one year we had an English preacher to teach us. About him I recall one thing only: he had a habit of notching the window sill with his jack-knife. This I did not like.

I also remember an older teacher who was rather small in stature. He was a real queer. He did not follow any program of studies and was not able to maintain any order, as the children did not seem to respect him.

YOUNG WELL-DIGGER

In 1912 he worked for J. Green at $30 per month. His job was to deepen a thirty foot well which had no water. There was one man working at the ground level and young Peter at the bottom. He dug the clay and filled a bucket. When the bucket was full the man on top used the winch to bring the bucket up and lowered another one down full of cribbing that had to be used to keep the sides of the well from caving in.

One afternoon before he could fill the bucket the man on top let go of the bucket with the cribbing. All this fell on the digger's head and he was nearly killed.

"I was winched up; I was crying. Mr. Green came along and when he found out what had happened, he fired the careless worker and the well digging was abandoned."

Harvesting in North Dakota

"When I was fifteen, my father told me that he made arrangements with other men in the district to have me accompany them to go harvesting. The boys went to the farmer where they had worked previously. I was the only new man. The fellows harnessed the teams they had worked with the previous year and went out to load the stooks. The only thing left for me was the spike pitcher's job. It was hard work as you had to pitch half the sheaves on the feeder, and when one was finished another stook-team would pull up and I had to climb up the load and keep going without any break. But I kept on working. I felt I had no alternative.

The work finished, somehow I was the only one to return home directly. I walked and it started to rain and kept on raining. I was soaking wet, but managed to maintain my direction. All of a sudden, as if from nowhere an animal jumped on my back. I was paralyzed, but I found out that it was our dog. Evidently in the dark I was walking past our farm. Life was not easy."

Peter Humeniuk, on completion of the elementary grades in Stuartburn, attended Dominion City school. And on completion of his high school in Teulon went teaching. He made a great contribution while a teacher in Dnister school at Gimli, organizing a dramatic club, a library and the building of a community hall a "narodnj dim". He was the first teacher to prepare students and encourage them to go to high school. Regrettably his strict moral standards were not accepted by some - he was very much anti-alcoholic drinking. He was dislodged from his position by a Hryc Vawkyk and his son-in-law, L. Zabloski, who were in business!

However, he accepted his problems with equanimity and no matter what the stress, he was a gentleman.

J. M. Storozuk: First Zhoda School Teacher

I was two years old in 1901, when we arrived in Canada to settle in the Stuartburn district. We lived there for two years. In the meantime, I was told, my father went around to the East of the present Vita region to select a homestead. Finally in late 1902 we were on our homestead. My parents considered themselves fortunate to be able to acquire 160 acres of land for $10.00

Our Home

Our house was built out of poplar logs that were available on our farm. So was fuel. The house was mud plastered. The roof was thatched with hay bundles. Any furniture we had was home-made, which consisted of a table, a stool, a big bench and a couple of beds.

We did not have a steel stove but one made out of stones and mud, which also included a similarly built bake oven. Over it was a platform like structure that could be used for sleeping.

There was no machinery to develop the "homestead". My parents brought with them a scythe for cutting hay, and a wooden cradle which when assembled could be used for harvesting grain. The grain was threshed with a flail on a specially made icy patch, and winnowed with the help of the wind.

Before the homestead produced anything father had to go away to work to earn the much needed "dollars".

As for food, it consisted of vegetables which were grown in our garden. Settlers who had a cow, had milk for the children, and now and then butter. Meat was mostly available in winter, for due to lack of freezers, people could not keep meat during summer.

As for clothing and shoes, these were bought. Mothers, however, sewed shirts and dresses for the children by hand. Yard goods were available in hamlet stores.

Life Dull

He continues:

More and more settlers arrived to settle on the non-too-productive soil. The soil was light and poorly drained. It was horribly stony, too.

One of the limiting factors was lack of knowledge of English and an opportunity of learning it. There was paucity of reading material, too. No Canadian newspapers in Ukrainian language were subscribed to. Some had a prayer book and the highly emotional book known as the "Prophecies of Michaljda". Many people were illiterate. During winter, generally speaking, life was dull.

When spring came the land was covered with water and swamps were created. Soon one could hear the croaking of the frogs that grew into a large size. The croaking of the frogs, the humming of the mosquitoes and the singing of the birds created an evening choir. And strange as it may be this "music" influenced me and I loved to listen to it, and believe that their "orchestration" developed in me a love of music.

Schooling

I was eight years old when during winter I started to attend school. And what a school it was! I went to a neighbour's home where there were two children, a boy and a girl. A winter boarder was the teacher and started to teach us to read and write in Ukrainian. I made good progress and soon I was able to read letters our neighbours received from the "Old Country"* and also to write letters for them to their relatives.

In 1911 the settlers erected the first school in the district and called it Kupchanko. I was eleven years old then. I started to attend school, but at the same time my attendance was limited as I was expected to help more and more with the chores and farm work. It was difficult for me in school, for my vocabulary consisted of very few words, some of them "unusable".

---

*Old Country - was Ukraine

In 1916 I completed grade six in Kupchanko school, and in 1917 I left for Winnipeg to get more education* - to take grade eight. I started late in the fall, after the farm work was done. I had a difficult time: inadequate command of English and no grade seven standard. I toiled through the year, and then the war was on and there was a lack of farm labour so I went to do farm work in the spring and as a consequence was given a high school entrance certificate.

Became A Soldier

After taking grade nine in the city, I was returning home and as I waited at the Union station for the train home I was approached to join the army, and I enlisted to receive military training. Since I was underage, I was discharged and thus able to complete my high school education.

In 1920 I got a permit to teach. My first school was Franko, twelve miles east of Vita. Then after completing my normal school I taught in Chmelnitski school north of Rossburn and Garland; Shevchenko and also Prawda close to Stuartburn. Then Lakedale in the Augusville area and that was all.

I was fortunate to meet a very talented girl, Anna Moroz. She was an artist and worked at Eaton's producing Eaton's catalogues. After we got married we went to Augusville where our darling Orysia was born. My Anna got ill, and we moved to Winnipeg.

Orysia grew up to be a nurse. After several difficult years of toil I finally worked in the Legislative Building in Winnipeg. I retired getting a small Provincial civil service pension.

Going to School East of Stuartburn

The Ukrainian settlers took early opportunity to organize schools to give their children a better chance to succeed in their new adopted land. Therefore, east of Stuartburn, the school district of Svoboda came into being. Five miles east on Mr. Kolisnyk's farm the rural school named Shevchenko was built and the post office also carried the same name. A local boy who attended that school provides us with information about school life and life in general of a boy who grew up in the district and later in life became a teacher and an outstanding community leader in Alberta.

Onifat Lukianchuk's Story

Vita, my home town, was predominantly a Ukrainian settlement. It consisted of a couple of stores and a number of homes scattered on each side of a track, which bisected the town from east to west. My home was built on the south side of the tracks.

---

*The Ukrainians in Winnipeg organized a residence for boys in a building - (still standing) - at the corner of Burrows and McGregor, and these boys who lived there were able to attend Sisler's Strathcona school.

The first school I attended was out in the country, about one mile north of the town. In those days, all the children walked to school since there were no buses or vans. In the summer, most of us tried to get to school early in the morning to have more time for playing. Our winters were very cold, many a time kids came to school with frozen noses and faces.

Our school was named Shevchenko. It was a one room school with big double desks for the children, a table and chair for the teacher and a blackboard on the front wall. At the back of the room stood a big wood heater around which we huddled and tried to warm ourselves on the cold days. We sat two to a desk and were supposed to observe complete silence during the study period. No one was allowed to turn around to talk to his or her neighbor, if however, one ventured to do so, his friend would immediately strike his nose with a pencil. On instruction from the teacher, therefore, most of the children were armed with long pencils.

As a beginner I spent a long time in grade one. The first text book I received when I came to school, contained such words as: conductor, passenger, engineer, brakeman, Queen Victoria, etc. The harder I tried to memorize these words the less I knew. Finally, when the new text books arrived, learning became easier and I began to make reasonable progress.

We had no grain elevators in town. The land in the district was not suited for good farming, only a little grain was grown and that was fed to the stock. Oxen were used for field work and travel. It took a long time to get anywhere or do any field work with oxen.

Dad used to buy and sell cattle. One time he bought a yoke of oxen. They were huge animals with big wide horns. He hitched them to a hayrack and told me to drive to our farm for a load of hay. Our hay farm was seven miles out of town, I was only eleven years old then. The idea of driving this yoke of oxen and bringing a load of hay all by myself was something special. I could brag to my pals about the big work I did. I started this trip with big expectations. Driving all the way to our farm, however, to get to the hay stack, the oxen had to cross a small creek. When I drove to it the huge beasts refused to ford the creek. Evidently they got scared of the water, and I had to return home without the hay, feeling ashamed and disappointed.

The farm work with the oxen was very slow and the farmers were eager to get horses, but horses were expensive and hard to get until Dad got a few carloads of wild horses (broncos) from Alberta. These he trained and sold to the farmers at reasonable prices. The bronco training was difficult and dangerous. Father trained one bronco at a time. He would hitch a bronco and a tame horse to a wagon. The tamed horse was a good trainer. It would start the run with a great speed and go for a mile or more. Such runs were made once a day and after a few days the horse would get trained.

We also had a contract to deliver mail from Vita. The delivery was made every Saturday with a buggy driven by a fast team of horses. Quite often when Dad was busy I drove the mail. I used to enjoy these trips, especially when I had extra passengers, people who having arrived by train would want to get home to Arbakka. For this they would pay me twenty-five cents a person; thus I learned to earn money at an early age.

Our church was also out in the country about one and a half miles northwest of the town. It was a Ukrainian Greek Catholic church. Later the parish split into two: the Ukrainian Greek Orthodox and the Ukrainian Greek Catholic and each built a church in town. I especially enjoyed going to the country church during Easter, since Easter then was a three day celebration, in which everyone took part. The children had much fun ringing the church bell, singing and playing (haiwky) "hahilka" Easter games.

After a few years the town began to increase. Besides the two churches, we got a co-op store, a creamery, a new school, a large community hall and more homes. The community hall became a centre for social and cultural activities. It contained a large Ukrainian library. It was here that I learned Ukrainian reading and writing and later took an active part in concerts and plays.

I wrote my departmental exam in Emerson. While there I saw in one of the stores a fiddle on display - priced at $5.00. I had always wanted to own a fiddle. Here was my chance. I skimped on my expenses and came back home with the fiddle. Here Mr. D. M. Ukryniuk was giving the students free violin lessons, so that is how I got my start in violin playing. Later it made it easier for me to teach a choir.

On the whole the early life at Vita was not easy. All the people were poor and money was hard to get. Everyone had to work hard, even the children. My home was quite far from a well, so for a few years I had to carry water by pails every day. We kids usually played such games as "piggy yamka". A number of us would stand around a hole with stout sticks, while one would be driving a can (pig) into the hole and we would be trying to prevent him from putting the can in the hole. When we got our new school then we played football and baseball.

Chapter 2

Reminiscences

The Bush Fire

Mrs. Anton Figus came to Canada with her parents, Mr. and Mrs. Nykola Cesmystruk in 1897. She grew up on the farm four miles west of Vita and when interviewed in 1976, remembered many events of pioneer days.

* * * * *

We had to live in temporary houses which our parents erected in a hurry. These were warm and fairly comfortable, but lacked headroom on the sides. They could not erect log houses similar to those in the Old Country as the poplar trees in this area were not of large growth.

The farm we settled on was virgin land as not even the stock of the Stuartburn ranchers had ever roamed in the area. One very dry year, the turf, the grass and the windfall were as dry as tinder and the people were most careful with fires. Late one fall, however, one started in the west, and fanned by the west wind, moved rapidly to the south-east, burning everything in its wake. The settlers facing disaster put their animals in their small stables as they watched the deer flee to the east and so did the foxes and the wolves. The rabbits, though seemed to bunch together for safety and emerged into the clearings by the thousand looking, it seemed, for a safe place. We children were petrified as we saw our parents move around nervously.

The settlers were helpless. Those whose houses had sod roofs were lucky for it was easier to keep them wet. My parents soaked the bed sheets in water and covered the thatch of our stable. Some people dug out pits and placed their tools and utensils in them to save them from burning. Children were particularly nervous and would run in and out of the house to check the stable to see if the animals inside were safe. On our farm someone left the stable door open to give the animals air and the rabbits rushed into the building by the hundred. A few even managed to get into our house, but they were not afraid us - they just huddled together in a corner and remained motionless.

The next day all one could see was open black stretches of land where the fire had gone through. Many settlers lost their haystacks - some lost their houses. Here and there in the open spaces one saw white patches as if snow covered - these were rabbits that had bunched together and were, it seems, afraid to dispurse. The greatest loss to the district was the burning off of the top soil. The land was left less productive.

THE GIRL FROM VITA
(Mrs. Anna Yakimischak)

I was born in Vita, Manitoba and received my early education in Shevchenko school which was located on my father's farm approximately a mile north of the present hamlet of Vita. It is likely that the hamlet may have grown to its present size at its original site, but with the coming of the railway the hamlet of Shevchenko, as the post office was then called, began to develop where the railway company established its stopping point.*

The Vita district was settled almost solidly by Ukrainian settlers. Things changed when the railway came in 1905. I remember when it was built and the track laid east of Emerson. There was one Anglo-Saxon who lived among them. He was a Mr. Wright, the section foreman. It was he who was responsible for changing the name of the railway station from Shevchenko to Vita. Consequently, the name of the post office was changed also. The name of the school remained unaltered. The school site, however, was changed when the school building was moved into town.

Of his family, my father, Iwan Kolisnyk, was the first to come to Canada. The reason for his coming was that he did not wish to do three years of compulsory military training for Franz Joseph and left for Canada arriving in Vita in 1898. He first selected a homestead and then went to work for the farmers west of the Red River. When my grandparents arrived he had earned enough money to by a cow and a yoke of oxen. Since my parents arrived during the fall term, it was too late to build a home and they lived in rented quarters.

Our farm seemed to be located along the trail used by the farmers in going to the forest reserve for suitable spruce and pine timber, mainly logs for buildings as the poplar trees in the area did not seem to be of adequate size for larger structures. These men used to stop at our farm very often sometimes staying overnight and sleeping on the floor.

When I was five years old, I started to go around to play with the other children. I spent so much time around the school that the then teacher, George Machula, suggested to my parents that I may as well attend regularly. I liked school. It was conducted on a bilingual basis and we were also taught the Ukrainian language the last half hour of the day. Gaining good comprehension in a remote area was a big problem: libraries were very small, newspapers were few and opportunities for communication with the other districts and Winnipeg were limited.

I was happy and satisfied with my environment, probably because I knew no other way of life. Vita was an active community and when the municipal hall was moved here to make the municipal office more central, it seems to me that it was used as a community hall too. Plays and concerts

---

*The railway was extended from Emerson Junction to Ridgeville in 1903 and connected with Sprague in 1907.

were staged and a library established. When the railroad went through, Vita became a very busy business centre.

No, I did not have to help mother with the other children. There were three of us in the family, each six years apart. True my parents lost a little girl who died of whooping cough. Until the coming of Dr. H. Waldon there was no doctor in this area to give any medical assistance.

How long did you attend school in Vita?

When Mr. Wasyl Jerowsky was teacher in the Shevchenko school he informed my parents that he could not devote too much time to helping me, particularly with such subjects as music and grammar and suggested that they send me to school in Winnipeg as there was no school nearby that I could attend and no high school in the district.

Did you go to school in Winnipeg?

Yes, after Christmas I went to Winnipeg. This was my first train ride. We arrived in Winnipeg and went to see Mr. George Machula who was working in some office. He suggested that I attend Norquay school.

I went to Norquay school and although I was only in grade six in the country they put me in grade eight. It was hard work coming from rural school with my language not too well developed and getting myself ready for the writing of the Entrance Examination which was then written at the end of grade eight.

Did the teachers help you? Who was the principal of the school?

The teachers were very kind and helped me. So did the other children to make it easier for me to get used to the demands of a larger school. I faced my examination with considerable concern, grammar and music worried me, particularly music. We had to take an oral test in music and the principal, Mr. Laidlaw, called us each in turn to his office to determine if we could sing the notes that were part of the examination. I did not do so well on my first attempt and he encouraged me saying, "try again". I am not certain, but I think I got an average in the nineties on my other subjects.

I started my grade nine in King Edward school and completed my high school at St. Johns. I lived with some good people and helped with the housework to get reduced rates for my keep.

How did you get along with the other students?

Although I came from the country, I was accepted by the students. We all came from more humble circumstances and were tolerant of each other.

On completing high school I received a permit to teach. I taught for several months at each of the following schools: Caliento, Zhoda and Whitemouth Lake and was accepted to attend Brandon Normal School. However, I was not paid my salary at the last named school and my parents, after helping me to attend school for some three years in Winnipeg, were not in a position to give me further help that year. So I did not receive teacher training. I married Dmytro Yakimischak, a teacher and a lawyer, who was elected M.L.A. from the Emerson constituency.

I Grew Up In Lord Roberts (Bukovyna) District

I grew up in Gardenton, four miles south of where my people settled in 1900. Our farm south of the present Gardenton, was covered with small bush and clearings, but there were not many large trees. I was five years old and there wasn't much I could do and there was no school. When I was eleven I attended Bukovyna school and the name was later changed to Lord Roberts. In that school at the start some 17 year-olds were in Grade I. One of our teachers spoke only English so we taught him and his five children Ukrainian. Besides him I remember Wasyl Kudryk and Nicholas Kasowan, who later ran a store in the hamlet.

We also had one brother in the family, William Jaman, who had higher education. He attended the gymnasium at Chernevtsi; but in Canada he could not teach as he did not know English; however, he knew Romanian, Latin, German and Ukrainian, later he learned English. Because he knew German he went to teach among the Mennonites in Gretna, or some other town. He taught there for several years.

At the start my parents went to Emerson to shop and my father used to go to work there. I also worked in Emerson for two years. Then I returned home.

Our district was settled by people who came form the Ukrainian province of Bukovyna and were closely related. They all belonged to the Orthodox Church, but we did not have our own clergyman, so missionaries came from the Russian Church in the United States. That's why our St. Demitios Church has connections with the Russian synod now.

In 1915, I married a member of the Tkachuk family in that church. There were many Tkachuks in the area. My husband did not want to farm so we went to Winnipeg where for many years he worked in a brewery.

Anna Zuk - Silver Cross Mother

The children and grandchildren of the "Sifton Settlers" who came to farm a large Ukrainian settlement east of Red River and Dominion City grew up to have a strong affinity, respect and love for their Ukrainian culture and heritage, and at the same time grew up to love their adopted land, and others the land of their birth - Canada. Their participation and the sacrifices of their men and women in W.W.II attest for this. The recognition Mrs. Anna Zuk received in 1994 was most fitting.

Anna Zuk was chosen a Silver Cross Mother on two occasions to carry out the function of lying a wreath during the Remembrance Day ceremonies. This she did representing Canadian Mothers, who like she, lost sons and relatives in W.W.I and II. In 1994, the Winnipeg Free Press recognized her by having her picture on the front page holding a picture of her son Emil who gave his life as a consequence of his participation in the Normandy invasion. Her son Bernie lost part of his arm fighting in Sicily. In 1994 he was in the military hospital in Chicago.

The honour to serve as Silver Cross Mother is bestowed on selected women who lay a wreath on Remembrance Day on behalf of all the mothers who lost sons in Canada's wars, wrote The Winnipeg Free Press (11/10/94).* This honour was bestowed on a child of Oleskiw settlers from the Ukraine.

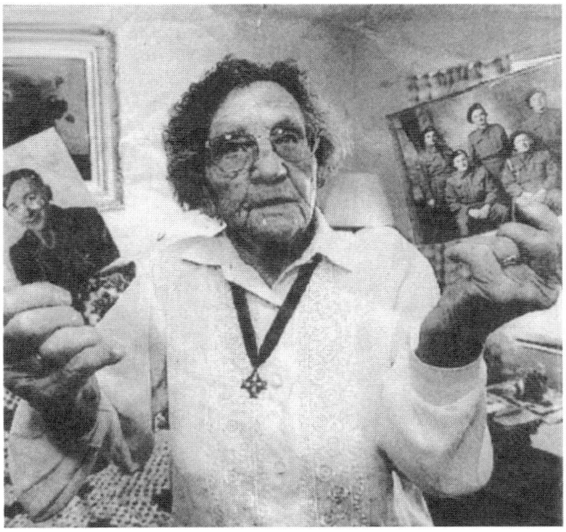

Fig. 1 Silver Cross Mother
Courtesy of Winnipeg Free Press 10 Nov/94

Her grief on Remembrance Day (when she was 92 years old) was the more intense for on D. Day on the beaches of Normandy when her son Emil was injured, Mrs. Anna Zuk lost her brother Nestor and two cousins.

Mrs. Anna Zuk is a daughter of the late Mr. and Mrs. Mateyj Prabizansky, the daughter of redoubtable pioneers of Stuartburn.

Mrs. Zuk grew up on a homestead three miles east of Stuartburn SW 1/4 23-02-06 E1. Started to attend Beckett school, (then called Svoboda) and transferred to Stuartburn. She, like other children of pioneers grew up with very little and work was often very hard. After she married her first husband, Eugene Prygroski, she stated, "I once spent an entire week cleaning a church." She earned $25.00 Life was hard on the farm particularly when the depression years set in.

A teacher of Beckett school where the three Prygroski children attended in the early thirties reported how hard Mrs. Zuk strived to glean a few pennies

* In 1998 Mrs. Anna Zuk was chosen to be a Silver Cross Mother in Ottawa.

to raise a family.

> I lived in a teacherage for part of the time and I recall Emil coming to me one day saying: "You are paying 10 cents a dozen for eggs. My mother will sell you larger and fresher eggs for 5 cents a dozen." I did buy her eggs, but did not have the heart to pay her less than 10 cents a dozen. Emil, as I remember him, was a very pleasant, well-mannered boy.

During our interview Mrs. Zuk proudly added: "My daughter Eva lives in California. Bernie has two daughters, one a doctor in Chicago and one a lawyer in Wisconsin."

Consequently, inspite of the antipathy towards the Ukrainian settlers in 1899 when Mrs. Zuk was born, they came to stay and inspite of toil and stress raised stalwart men and capable women, and helped Canada to become a great country.

Mrs. Olinek: 36 Years in the Same House

For 36 years I lived in the house where I was married to a section foreman. Rev. E. Andruchowich married us. The train stopped long enough for him to perform the marriage ceremony and he left for Winnipeg.

My parents lived four miles north of the village and I attended school there. There was little a girl could do but work on the farm or become a dishwasher or a domestic in Winnipeg. I was married at sixteen.

Now I am not well and neither is my husband: I live in the low-rental home and he is here in the personal care home - not well at all after 47 years as a trackman. Life was happy in this community and now it is sad...People liked each other and now no one comes to visit us. We had a very fine community centre, I took part in plays, we had a good library, but it was destroyed by fire. I can't read now. My husband took an active part in the community also and organized the baseball club.

Mr. Olinek:

I looked after 10 miles of track and through the years had good men work for me like Mr. Machula, Mr. Moroziuk and others. We had a car. I bought a Ford for $300. Now I get a pension of $215 from C.N.R. and an old age pension. We can live well, but - no health, no energy. Had to be at work every day you know. Work in winter was hard at times; this is low-lying land and there was a lot of shimming to do, but I had a good record - no accidents. I started to work with a pump car...pumping seven miles against the winter wind was hard, oh...!

Mrs. Olinek:

This community was lucky to have Dr. Waldon: He was a blessing to the people in Vita and the district. He never spared himself - he operated on me.

My children are far away: the oldest son, a train conductor in Troy, Michigan, a daughter in Vancouver; another son in Toronto, C.N. conductor and one in Sioux Saint Marie - Algoma Steel. We are here waiting. They visit us.

The Bookbinder's Daughter

My grandfather, Nicholas Kohut, was among the first group of Oleskiw settlers who came out in 1896. In that year he selected his homestead, the S.W. 1/4 of 22. He came out alone, but in 1900 he was joined by my father, Joseph, who came to Canada to avoid compulsory military training. Then the whole family came out. My father, after working out and living with my grandparents during four winters, bought a farm, got married and started to develop his farm - it was not a homestead. My parents raised three girls and two boys. The girls are all here and the boys in Toronto.

My parents got along fairly well. The farm, though stony, provided them with a good living. My father was a man of many skills and made many of his own tools and equipment, such as rakes, axe helves and others. He was probably the only one in the area who did bookbinding. We have many books of his binding. He seemed to bind religious books, in the main, as he was a devote churchman. He was a cantor in the church and wrote about early church history of the district.

There was quite a community here and a pioneer cemetery was established in the middle of section 22, in the inner corner of my grandfather's farm. It was along a trail that ran to the northeast of Stuartburn and then directly east to the Shevchenko district, which later became Vita. Since it was too far from a road allowance, and no ditch was close by, the cemetery was poorly drained and always wet. Finally this cemetery was abandoned and another one started. There was also a cemetery of the Independent Church, but it is plowed over now.

As a child I attended Svoboda school which was renamed Beckett by the official trustee. Then I worked at home until my first marriage when we bought this land, John Probizansky's homestead. He moved out to start a store and to be a post-master in Stuartburn. For many years he was the community leader in the Stuartburn area.

My father died when he was 93 and the boys took over his farm. They sold it for $700. and the German family that bought it resold it later for $15,000.

We are also reaching the age when we cannot work our farm, but we hate to give up the garden - I love my flowers.

Nicholas Danylchuk of Zhoda

One spring day in 1978, Mr. Nicholas was interviewed in his home in Zhoda, Manitoba. We found him splitting stove-length poplar wood and making a neat pile. He was in good health, but complained about impaired hearing.

Consequently, he spends much time reading and watching T.V. He and Mrs. Danylchuk live with their oldest son in a comfortable bungalow. He is a happy pioneer, but decries the fact that the young people have left the district and that the once socially active community, now is practically none existent - only the Post Office helps to remind the people of the early days. He reported:

"In the village of Pilipche in Ukraine, there wasn't much future for me. If I were to get married and live with my parents, there wasn't enough land to support two families. I was eighteen years old and would have to do military training. We discussed the matter with my parents and they got enough money together to pay my passage to Canada.

I arrived in Canada before the First World War and my uncle, who had a farm at Zhoda, suggested that I go out to Saskatchewan to seek employment. When I worked for a farmer in the Weyburn area, the war started. I was afraid that since I was not a Canadian citizen that I may be forced to go back home; but I didn't want to go back. One reason why I left home was that I did not want to serve in Franz Joseph's army. I could not join the Canadian army, so I worked for the same farmer for four years.

During my four years in Weyburn, I learned English and this helped me. Now I am forgetting the language as I do not use it often.

In 1921 I returned to the Zhoda, I bought a farm for $600., built a small house and stable and started farming. By this time I was interested in a local girl and married Mary Baysarowich and we continued to develop this farm.

We started to work our farm with oxen: they were slow and the flies tormented them. Winter travel wasn't bad, but in spring and summer it took a long time to go to Vita across the swamps. (Our M.L.A., D. Yakimischak wasn't able to help the area very much. We paid taxes and had few improvements. Bracken did not seem to care). Finally we got horses and had 80 acres under cultivation. We had a mixed farming operation.

At one time I thought that if Ukraine would remain independent - and it was for a short period after the First World War - that I would return; but finally we sank our roots in this Zhoda soil and here I am in my 85th year.

We had difficult years on the farm and the high taxes nearly drove us out. At one time the taxes on our quarter-section reached $100. per year. There was no control over the official trustee and school taxes were very high.

The land here was low and the drainage was poor. We sold cord wood, raised cattle and sold cream. We took our cream to Vita.

We raised five children, four boys and one girl. The oldest boy is unmarried and he runs the farm. My daughter, Stephanie, Mrs. John Chopek, lives across the road. One boy is a section foreman in Marchand, one a school teacher in Lorette and the third works in Winnipeg. They all attended Devon school. The teacher had finished university. Two boys married French girls. One had to get the permission from the French bishop to marry a French girl. The third one married a Ukrainian girl and his children can speak Ukrainian."

Mrs. Agnes Stefiuk

My early life was difficult: I do not remember my parents. The good people of the village brought me up. I was in my native village during the First World War and experienced extreme hardships. I am fortunate that i was able to get an elementary school education. My brother, Iwan Katereniuk left for Canada before World War I and worked as a section hand. When the war was over, he sent me money and I came to Canada in 1923. I was 23 years old then.

The next year I got married. My husband was a good man. He even repaid my brother the money he spent in getting me to Canada.

My sister was to come to Canada with me, but before leaving she went to a fortune-teller who told her that she would die on the boat and be buried at sea. So she would not go.

My husband was good to me and now I often cry and say, "Why don't you take me to you?"

When we lived in Arbakka, Mr. Jerowsky was our neighbor. He taught school and had a post office and a small store.

My children went to school in Arbakka and Vita and also Fort Frances. My son was very ill and I took him to the doctor in the U.S.A. I have good children - some people have difficulty with their children. My daughter is a teacher and my son has a good job in Portage la Prairie.

My children did not want me to live alone, that's why I am in this home. A teacher rents my house. I still go to church, but my trouble is with my eyes. That makes it difficult for me to correspond with my cousins in Zalischyky. She has written to me often, but now I am unable to answer her letters. Here is one letter I received from the Ukraine:

"My first words are, Christ is Born! "Krystos Rodyvshia". Let us praise Him! "Slavite".

> My dear Mrs. Stefiuk:
>
> I received your letter on St. Jordan's Day and was so delighted that I kissed it as if I were kissing you, for you visited me with this letter and have not forgotten about me. You wrote me that there is a shortage of water in your area. Here we have no snow, a little fell but has now melted. Well, we have finished our holidays and visited most of our relatives, but they, like we, are not very happy. We can't sing carols, because we are old; and the young people do not know how to sing carols - but they do not need any training to be able to drink whisky. They can do it without carols. At one time we enjoyed happiness, our children used to visit us and bring their supper and we all had our supper together and sang carols. And now who comes to see me!? At one time, we at least had older people as neighbors, and now we are old and have no place to visit. If we at least had our grandchildren nearby, we would be happier. This way we stay in the house and have plenty to think about. Some of the strangers would like to come, but all they would want is that you give them something as they would like to take something away - because older people do not need much.

You are asking me if I received the jacket. I wrote you some time ago - it was during the old year - and told you what things I received...and a dress of some kind, maybe you call it a jacket, but it is sleeveless. People do not wear things like that here...

Mrs. Stefiuk I wrote you some time ago - either you did not get my letter or the letters crossed enroute. I live in hope that your health will improve daily and that you will be able to write longer letters, you always write me such sort ones. Mrs. Stefiuk, why do you feel so depressed and tend to lose hope? It is not good to think like that. There are many people older than you who seem to have a better attitude to life. Mrs. Stefiuk, we are under the care of the Lord. The Almighty never abandons anyone and he will not forget us. All we older people are not fairly treated by our children as they do not seem to love us any more. So we have to accept things as they are. When we talk about our parents, we often cry; but as far as we are concerned...maybe not even the dog will utter a bark, when we pass away.

Mrs. Stefiuk, I have never been as ill in my life as I have been recently and only got out of bed two days. ago. I had the grippe and was in bed for five weeks. My husband was ill for two weeks. It is difficult to be ill when one is old...But what can one do? One seems to catch all the diseases spread around, but one has to adjust to things as they are, and continue to believe in God's grace.

Letter received after an interview in Vita, Manitoba in 1973.

Theodore Kutsak

I came to Halifax in 1905 directly from Hamburg. The ticket from Hamburg to Winnipeg cost me 140 levs. ($1.00 American was equal to about 2 1/2 levs. T.K.) We were dumped in East Selkirk and had to walk to Winnipeg. We spent the night in the Immigration Hall. Then we started for Gardenton, it was night time when on crossing a railway bridge, we were attacked and robbed. We, however, continued and walked to Gardenton to my uncle John Odokijchuk's place.

I came to Canada to earn money, and return home but coming to Gardenton, I got married. To earn money, I used to go across the Boundary to work for a farmer in the U.S.A.

In 1908, when George Shepit moved to British Columbia, I brought his NE 1/4 5 - 1 - 9E and then the one in township 6.

My farm had no stones and had about five acres ploughed. I sold cord wood in Sundown. During the harvest season I went working for farmers in Ninga and Boisevain. We sold cream and fence posts across the line in the U.S.A. On the start I worked my farm with horses and second hand machinery.

Province of Manitoba
Province of Manitoba
31
Province of Manitoba
Province of Manitoba
Province of Manitoba
Province of Manitoba
32
Province of Manitoba
Province of Manitoba
Province of Manitoba
Josef Happy-chuk
33
Province of Manitoba
Province of Manitoba
Josef Happy-chuk
Province of Manitoba
34
Province of Manitoba
Province of Manitoba
Province of Manitoba
Steve Bugera
35
John Waskul
Petro Wepruk
Iwan Wyrbicki
Samuel Boychuk
36
Nikolai Alexiuk
Michal Bojczuk
Province of Manitoba
Province of Manitoba
30
Province of Manitoba
Province of Manitoba
School Land
School Land
29
School Land
School Land
Province of Manitoba
Province of Manitoba
28
LGD of Stuartburn
Michal Rogowski
Province of Manitoba
Province of Manitoba
27
John Rogowski
Michael Boychuk
Mike Waskul Jr.
George Alexiuk
26
Hudson's Bay Company
Hudson's Bay Company
Maike Franko
Stephen Franko
25
Tedor Werenko
Nykola Shypit
Province of Manitoba
Province of Manitoba
19
Province of Manitoba
Province of Manitoba
Hnat Rogowski
Leonty Yocko
20
Nastia Luk
Wasyl Boyczuk
Province of Manitoba
Province of Manitoba
21
Province of Manitoba
Province of Manitoba
Province of Manitoba
Province of Manitoba
22
Province of Manitoba
Province of Manitoba
Province of Manitoba
Province of Manitoba
23
Province of Manitoba
Maksam Dakushk
Olexa Andrusek
John Luka-sievicz
24
Nikola Andrusiak
Mardary Andrusiak
Iwan Strutz
Province of Manitoba
18
Province of Manitoba
Province of Manitoba
Province of Manitoba
Province of Manitoba
17
Province of Manitoba
Peter Hnatiuk
Province of Manitoba
Michal Czobotar
16
Wasyl Dyley
Prockup Woncha-lenko
Province of Manitoba
Peter Boychuk
15
Harry Czubey
John Bodnar-chuk
Michelo Shypit
Wasel Kosteniuk
14
Petro Skrumeda
Iwan Skrumeda
John Boychuk
Wasyl Andrusiak
13
Province of Manitoba
Metro Skrumeda
Wasyl Sandul
Hrynko Perchaluk
7
Wasyl Bodnar-czuk
Onufry Bodnar-czuk
Hudson's Bay Company
Hudson's Bay Company
8
Hudson's Bay Company
Hudson's Bay Company
John Chobotar
Nick Makowski
9
Wasyl Malenko
Todor Panteluk
Alex Bilawczuk
George Chobotar
10
Mitro Bilawczuk
Gregory Belowchuk
School Land
School Land
11
Fred Kutzak
School Land
Nykolay Tokorow
Nick Lewenec
12
Iwan Andrusiak
Olekse Chobotar
Prokip Bodneriuk
Michael Waskul
6
Georgie Nykoluk
Dmytro Waskal
Mike Hryhorec
George Czornopski
5
Leon Lapuszniak
John Swerdylak
Nykola Kaczur-owski
Mike Chobotar
4
George Kosher-owsky
John Jaman
Dmytro Guszalak
George Schepit
3
Gregori Dzassul
Frank Penteluk
Simeon Szpot
Maria Szkrumeda
2
Todyr Sidor
Nykola Szypit
1
George Skrumeda
George Franchuk

Fig. 2 Township 1, Range 9E – Sirko Area

Sirko oxen.

Cutting hay at Sundown (Credit Shevchenko (4-12) School).

Sirko farmers changed to horses and an old mule (John Gushalak standing).

Fig. 3a

Chapter 3

The Younger Group
The Caliento-Born Violin Maker

John Hoplock, in his day, was the outstanding violin and prosthesis maker in Winnipeg. He was the man who made replicas of Gaurnerius 1763 violin in addition to four replicas of Stradivarius and others. As a specialist orthopedic limb-maker he operated a Main Street shop for 42 years.

John Hoplock was born in Caliento, MB, April 10, 1904 where his parents settled on a homestead. His father's name was Henry Hopaliuk and his mother's name was Zocia. She was from the Baliuk home. They came to Canada from the village of Zalischyky, Western Ukraine. After a few years he became dissatisfied with the land in the Caliento area, and bought a farm east of Oakbank.

Henry Hopaliuk was a hard-working man and a demanding father to a point of being cruel. One cold, stormy day he had John, then 19 years old, go on horseback into the bush to cut cordwood.

At nightfall when the horse returned home alone, John's brother went to look for him. Evidently, John fell off a galloping horse and fractured his leg.

John stayed home for several days, but the pain was unbearable. His brother took him to Hazelbridge, but they had no money for a train ticket. A freight train came along and the trainman took them into the caboose. Once in Winnipeg they went by street car to the General Hospital. Two well-known surgeons found that gangrene had set in and amputated his leg below the knee, then they arranged for him to study making artificial limbs with a Winnipeg limb maker. He got so good that he went into business on his own. When a bank accountant, T. G. Smith, went to him for a better limb, he suggested that John change his name from Hopaliuk to Hoplock. His business was good and he also became a violin repairman for the Winnipeg Symphony Orchestra and a violin maker. He made an exact replica of a 1793 Joseph Gaurnerius violin:

> I've been told I could sell it for $5,000, but I plan to leave it to my son. (The family was musical and his son was a member of the Winnipeg Symphony Orchestra, but died as a result of a car accident when only seventeen)

Marjorie Gillies added this information:

> Hoplock says replicas of the four Stradivarius, circa 17th century David Teakler and four Gaurnerius violins he has crafted from imported....woods are to be found among collections held by renowned North American violinists today.

As far as wood is concerned:

> Personal curiosity also led him to make a violin bows from a hawthorne branch. The first one he plucked from the roadside near Winnipeg Beach.

Then:

> During the next 42 years, until his retirement he made 5000 prostheses for amputees who continue to call him from across the country, the U.S.A. and Great Britain when the artificial limbs needed repairing.

He was especially proud of this case:

> Hoplock remembers one special limb, he made for Sir Hugh John Macdonald shortly before he died, as the lightest-weight prosthesis he ever made. "It weighted only 3½ pounds," he recalls. "Macdonald was so frail at the time he couldn't cope with a regular artificial limb after he lost his leg."
> Age is irrelevant to Hoplock. Nor is time spent in his workroom ever less than a labor of love.[1]

Fig. 3 Hoplock's instruments brought sweet sounds to many musicians over the years.

(It is interesting that Sir Hugh John Macdonald opposed people with names like Hopaliuk from coming to Canada.)

William Prochuk's Violin Magic

Before my parents settled in Zhoda, they had pioneered in Montana, but were lonely being away from Ukrainian people and made a change. They settled in a stony - marshy area and I grew up in Zhoda.

As a pre-schooler I was fascinated by the sound of the violin. In those days the only two instruments one could listen to were the violin and the cymbalon. These two instruments provided the music for all social gatherings and celebrations in the community.

---

1 Marjorie Gillies, Winnipeg Free Press, January 9, 1990, p.25

By the age of ten I was completely possessed with a desire to have a violin of my own. My father, however, did not want me to be a fiddler as he did not have a good opinion of some of the musicians that went around the country playing at weddings and dances. He considered them to be worthless, dissolute creatures, and would never allow his son to pursue their kind of life. My entreaties, therefore, earned nothing but flat denials. In desperation I began mentally to explore other avenues, and came up with one alternative: to make my own fiddle.

To make a fiddle, I had to work in secrecy, which was not always easy. Eventually, I had the instrument finished, in a sort of way. It was a crude monstrosity - its most important part was screen wires used for strings. The bow was a dry ferule. But it gave forth sounds which, to me, were not much unlike those of a violin. I used to steal behind our woodshed and forget the whole world as I sawed upon my creation. Although I produced only weird sounds, they were music to me.

One late summer afternoon my father discovered me enjoying my pastime behind the woodshed. His initial anger gave way to amazement at the evidence of my resourcefulness. The incident was highly fortunate, because not long after this episode, a violin arrived in the mail and I found myself, in the "seventh heaven". As I recall it came from Eaton's and cost five dollars. The bow and resin were included in the price.

I knew nothing about tuning the violin and my father kept admonishing me to be careful and not draw the strings too taut lest they snap. I studied the folder that came with the package and since I was only in grade two my knowledge of English was not good enough to understand the instructions. However, I had watched fiddlers at parties and weddings, tuning up their instruments and I tuned mine as best I knew how. I looked at the Eaton's catalogue and tried to have the pegs stand as they were on the violin in the catalogue; all the while being very careful not to tighten the strings too much.

It worked. I drew the bow across the strings and the sound filled my ears. I liked it although mother protested that I was doing something wrong.

Mother loved to sing. She sang Ukrainian folk songs - and she knew so many of them by heart. She, therefore, became my music teacher: she sang and I tried to have my violin make the sounds to reproduce her songs. It was a slow process discouraging to my mother, no doubt, but in time tunes emerged and I acquired a small collection of musical tunes I could play.

According to my earliest recollection, when I was able to play my violin, I became a favorite with my aunt and uncle who lived nearby. Now that I was a "violinist" my social standing was greatly enhanced in their household. One Sunday afternoon during my first serious recital at their house, one of the young men who frequently visited there (in my uncle's household there were five lovely teen-age daughters - a good reason why young men flocked to his home) watched me intently. When I finished the selection I was playing, he picked up my fiddle to play a tune of his own. He was startled. I soon discovered the reason: The fiddle was improperly tuned. He tuned my violin and played a tune, but when I tried to play again I could not produce a tune. This crushed me completely and totally. I discovered that I would have to relearn everything: I was humiliated to the limit!

Fortunately, my gloom didn't last very long for after working hard I was able to play again all the tunes I knew. I had a good ear for music and this helped me to keep the fiddle in tune. I persisted in spending all my available time at playing, but I could play only by ear and I wanted more. Of course, all those in our district who played the fiddle or the cymbalon played only by ear, but I wanted to do better, I wanted to learn to play from notes. In time I obtained from somewhere a book of instruction and thus began my slow but careful study of music on my own: I succeeded and again, I was ushered into another world of wonder and beauty.

At that time there lived a man in the neighboring community whose skill as a fiddler was well-known. His name was Mr. Gonta. I, therefore, aspired to become as good a musician as he, and to belong in his class of fiddlers. He was, to me, a great magician: With the touch of his nimble fingers the violin would warble like a bird or sigh like a gentle breeze; laugh like a happy child or cry like a tortured soul. His music was gaiety and sadness, while in comparison mine was still, at times only a series of squeaks and screeches.

However, I made progress and several years later it so happened that I played at a community gathering, at which Mr. Gonta was present. By this time I had become quite good as a fiddler. I noticed that Mr. Gonta listened to my playing with a great deal of interest, and then during the intermission he came up to me, clapped me gently on the shoulder, and said - his voice subdued with emotion: "Boy, some day you are going to become a great violinist. Keep at it, don't ever give it up."

Although I did not become a great violinist, yet at the time, I think I was the happiest boy in the world. What is more, the music of a violin has never ceased to be a source of magic to me. And during my rural school teaching, my violin helped me to teach singing in school.*

* * * * *

Though William Prochuk was born in Montana where his family first settled, but grew up in Zhoda in south-eastern Manitoba where his people moved to be with their relatives, he did not start school early yet he developed his English by using the Eaton's catalogue as a reader. He, therefore, had a knowledge of English when the school in the district opened up.

> I was given authority to teach in Zhoda by Dr. R. Fletcher. However, my greatest difficulty was that I could not communicate with the pupils - they didn't under-

*From an interview with William J. Prochuk, 1978

stand what I said. Fortunately among them there was one, Bill Prochuk who understood me. He, therefore, became my interpreter. I would say what I wanted the class to know to Bill, and he always started to address the whole class in Ukrainian: "Vin Kazhy". For a long time I didn't know what he meant, but in time I got to understand that it was, "he says". By the end of the year I did not need a interpreter. The progress the grade one children, ages six to fifteen made was unbelievable and I was pleased with myself.**

* * * * *

I was principal of the Shevchenko school at Vita and boarded at Drul's. One of my students, Bill Prochuk also boarded there. He was a fine fellow. However, as far as I was concerned, he had one fault: he practised playing the violin as he was taking a correspondence course. He practised for an hour each evening religiously, and his practicing used to annoy me at times, but I decided I wasn't going to lose my temper. The only respite I had from his violin practice was when he took his violin to play for his girl friend.***

William Prochuk taught school in several rural areas of Manitoba. He married one of Nazar Bodnarchuk's girls and raised a fine family. One boy joined the Airforce and during one flight lost his life forced to land in the Interlake area.

William Prochuk retired as teacher from the Winnipeg School District.

The Zhoda Mudrys

As more settlers left for Canada from the Ukrainian province of Halychyna, news reached Dmytro Mudry of Humenetz in the Lviv district and in 1905 with his wife Elesaveta and children John, Palahia, Matthew and Anne they left for Winnipeg. His son Hryhorij remained to complete his cabinet making apprenticeship in Vienna.

After four years in Winnipeg, the Mudry family left for the Zhoda. Dmytro and two sons built a home on the mosquito infested Rat River. Farming was difficult, so Dmytro, a blacksmith by training, started a smithy on the Rat. His problem was to get a supply of coal for his forge. He, therefore, depended on the harder dry wood.

In Ukraine Dmytro did not have a chance to attend school so as a teenager he went to the village "chanter" (drak) to learn to read and write. To pay for his training, he used to go to the river in the village, get his feet in the water and as the leeches started to attach themselves to his feet, he plucked them off and sold them to the village "leech doctor".

Knowing the value of education, he with other homesteaders, decided to build a school. Franko school was built by him and his sons, John, and

---

**As related by Mr. Adrian Ashley.

***Eldon Simms, erstwhile Inspector of Schools

Hryhorij, the cabinet maker.

As the local homesteaders wanted and needed to establish the requisite community facilities. Michael Bicerovich donated land for the school; Mr. Andrusik provided land for the church, and Mr. Gigoluk, for the cemetery.

The Franko school became an important centre for cultural activities: Plays and concerts were staged in it. Dmytro's daughter took a leading part in an operetta, Natalka Poltavka.* This was an ambitious project for a small community.

Dmytro Mudry who came to the Zhoda district in 1909 passed away in 1914. His descendants found it difficult to adjust to farming in the area and left, but his widow stayed in the Rat area for several years; her younger children remained on the farm with her. But Zhoda farms did not have the holding capacity for others.

Her son John stayed on his farm, until 1921 when he moved to Winnipeg. He sold his farm and bought a home in Winnipeg.

Hryhorij, the cabinet maker retained ownership of his and his father's homestead renting the land to Mr. Tymofichuk and found employment in Transcona and C.N.R. in Rainy River. Finally he built a house in Winnipeg.

Matthew and his sister Anne left for Los Angeles. Anne, a nurse by training, who came to Canada as a child in now 96 and lives in her own home in San Francisco.

Hryhorij and Theodora had five children: Natalie, Eugenie, Elesaveta, Palahia and Nestor BSc.E. He was chief of Water Management in Manitoba.

Fig. 4 Mudry Home Beside Rat River.

* It appears that a teacher, Michael Kadyniuk who played the violin trained the actors.

The Sandilands Group

Adding to the younger generation group we include four people from the Sandilands area. Sandilands was a railway stop and steady employment was available there for men as members of the railway track maintenance crew. Miss Slavka Harasymyk was the daughter of a section foreman, finished high school in Winnipeg and was employed as a dental aide in Toronto.

A Mr. Danylchuk was in business in the hamlet and was able to give his son Alexander an opportunity to complete high school in Winnipeg. He then became a high school principal in Pine River and then changed to medicine. As a physician he had a successful practice in Canora, Saskatchewan.

Mr. J. Olchowecki was a track maintenance man. Two of his sons completed high school in Winnipeg with Peter becoming a school teacher and was for many years principal of Shevchenko school and later transferred to Winnipeg. His younger brother, Alexander, was a student at St. Andrew's College and then changed to study science at the University of Manitoba, and after attaining his doctorate was on the staff of the University of Manitoba as a Biology professor.

The first three were in residence at the P. Mohyla Institute in Winnipeg.

TABLE 2 EARLY SETTLERS:

TOWNSHIP 03, RANGE 08 EPM

ZHODA AREA SETTLERS

BAYSAROWICZ, JOSEPH	SW21	1908	ANDRUSEK, STEFAN	SE30	1903
GOLDA, FRANK	SW21	1929	NOWAK,STEFAN	NE30	1908
WINTONIW, NYKOLA	NW22	1940	RUDIJ, JOSEPH	NW30	1909
JOSEPHSON, ARNI	SE22	1903	BALA, HRYNKO	SE31	1916
IWACHA, HRYNKO	SW22	1930	KACAN, WASYL	SW31	1911
STECKI, JOHN	NW23	1924	IWACHA, HRYNKO	NE22	1903
BRIDGEMAN, WILLIAM BRYAN	SW24	1920	SYCIUK, NYKOLA	NW32	1903
YANCZYK, ANTHONY	NE26	1912	WOLICKI, IWAN	SE32	1903
NARTH, MICHAEL	NW26	1983	TRACZ, ELKO	SW32	1903
TURNOPOLSKI, TONY	NE27	1922	SMERCHYNSKI, MICHAL	NE33	1911
YURKOWSKY, JOHN	NW27	1925	IWACHOW, MICHAL	NW33	1910
SMYRICHINSKY, TONY	SE27	1930	PANKOW, TANAS	SE33	1914
SZOLOOGIN, MERIN	NE28	1903	WERBENIUK, ANNA	SW33	1909
DZOGOLYK, IWAN	NW28	1903	PLECZIJ, PANKO	NE34	1903
ROHATYNSKI, NYKOLA	SE28	1905	JURKOWSKI, MICHAL	NW34	1903
ZALUCKI, HRCHIR	SW28	1903	TERNOPILSKY, YANKO	SE34	1903
TYSOSKI, KASMER	NE29	1951	KACZOR, JOSEPH	SW34	1903
FOSTY, PETER	NW29	1951	ZACHARKIW, IWAN	NE35	1921
WINTONIW, KAZMER	SE29	1951	ZACHARUK, ANDRY	NW35	1921
FOSTY, JACOB	SW29	1951	STELMACH, SEMKO	SE35	1909
FAREENA, SIMEN	SW30	1908	SMERECZYNSKI, NASTOR	SW35	1921
CIUPA, BLASZKO	NE30	1904	HARASYM, HARRY	NE36	1931
FARINA, JOHN	NW30	1903	HAWRYZKO, HYRNKO	NW36	1910
FAREENA, SIMEN	PSW3	1903	HAWRYCHKO, MIKE	SW36	1930

The Boy from Arbakka - Peter Onysko

Like many others from the Ukrainian Province of Bukovyna, my parents filed for a homestead in Township one R7 north of the 49th parallel. That part of the country was known as the "prairie". It was low lying land where there was plenty of hay, but no wood for building or firewood: It had to be brought in from the east. What was more, there was no school I could attend. And I wasn't able to walk to any distant school as I developed bone-infection in one of my legs. Then when I was ten years old my parents bought land in the Arbakka area and we moved into what was once a small Icelandic settlement. Arbakka in Icelandic means the bank of a river. The river, of course, was the Roseau River flowing from the U.S.A. in a north-west direction into the Red River.

In Arbakka I started to attend school. But I was ten years old and totally illiterate. Fortunately the teacher in our school was a young girl from out Cartwright way, Miss Cummings. She was a smart woman and took pity on me and she helped me along as she did other children. I was fortunate that with her help by the time I was fourteen, I was prepared to write the Entrance Examination.

To be able to write the Entrance examination, I had to pay a two-dollar fee and go to write the examination at Vita, a distance of eight miles from our home. It was too far to walk, so it was suggested that I ride horseback. I started early and was in time to report for my examination - I think I wrote two. I fed my horse at noon and ate my lunch and went back to the school.

However, when I got out at four to ride my black mare home, she was nowhere to be found. Some Vita rascals let her loose and she wandered away. I looked for my horse for awhile and then decided to walk home. Having a weak leg, it wasn't easy, but I made it. I came home, but there was no Dolly. Then in about half an hour my Dolly arrived in the yard. I did pretty well to beat the horse home.

Our life in Arbakka was different. There was little chance to use the English language and not much to do for recreation. My father spoke little English. But he was a roadmaster, I think they called him that. One day he and an older Icelander started to scrape a ditch to drain a wet spot into the Roseau. To do this they had to plow a few furrows first, as there were many stones. Well, Canada is a democratic country, and the man in charge, my father, decided to consult Helgi. And he asked: "You bastard think, one plough, two ploughs?" He meant furrows, he also meant, "better".

Yes, we lived close to the U.S.A. and people used to take their cream across to Caribou. They also drove the cattle they had for sale across the "line". We had one cow that was trained and when father selected the steers and heifers he wanted to sell he would bell the red cow and start the cattle out of the yard. She knew what to do and started out for the U.S.A., the rest followed her. Once they arrived in Caribou, he took the bell off, she wandered away for home leaving the rest in the enclosure. People chasing cattle across the stateline had to be careful not to get caught by a patrol man. However, if he noticed that the cattle were on their own he would not bother chasing them back. And come next year, the red cow did the trick again.

I remember going across the line on my own one Sunday. I had a dime and decided to go to Caribou to buy myself some candy. It was a few miles to go, but I bought myself a treat and brought some home for the other children.

* * * * *

Having completed my Entrance Examination which qualified me to commence high school, the problem arose: would I go away from home to live in Vita, Emerson or Dominion City. My father subscribed to the Ukrainian Voice and knew that it was possible to go to Saskatoon to live in the Mohyla residence for Ukrainian children and attend the Nutana Collegiate. Since he was doing well with the sale of cattle and the shipping of cream, and I did not appear strong enough to work on the farm, it was decided that I proceed to Saskatoon. A Drul boy went there and so did Onifat Lukianchuk. I, therefore, attended school in Saskatoon where I completed high school and a teacher-training course.

While in the Mohyla residence, I was fortunate to meet a lovely girl, Mary Chepil, whose parents farmed south of Portage la Prairie. She was a classmate of mine. We were both able to get a contract to teach in Saskatchewan, so we got married. Later we moved back to Manitoba and taught in several schools, Shevchenko and Cook's Creek. Then a friend of ours got us a school in the Riverton area. He was no other than Michael Ewanchuk, and we taught in Tarno school. It was a two room school. Mary was able to teach and to raise two children, Donald and Nadia. With Mary gone Nadia Evans looks after me now. I was also principal of Riverton school and finished my career on the staff of Division No.1. My son Donald has been a scholarship winner, got the Athlone award and now works out of Ottawa. Nadia, a teacher, has a fine propensity for art and receives encouragement from her professor husband. My son-in-law, Evans is teaching at the University of Winnipeg.

John Panchuk - Didn't Forget His Roots

Mr. John Panchuk was another Canadian-born who contributed to the enrichment of written records about Ukrainians in Canada.

> Born in Gardenton, Man., in 1904, Mr. Panchuk came to Detroit in 1916 with his parents William and Irene Panchuk, originally immigrants from Bukovyna, Ukraine. In 1926, he graduated summa cum laude from the University of Michigan, and two years later finished that university's law school. In 1929 John Panchuk began practicing law in Detroit.
>
> Appointed assistant attorney general for the state of Michigan in 1937; in 1941 he joined the Federal Life and Casualty Company as general legal counsel.

Fig. 5 John Panchuk

In the early 1940's Mr. Panchuk with another Canadian, John W. Ewanchuk spearheaded efforts to create and organize the Ukrainian Congress Committee of America.

All his life Mr. Panchuk studied the life and literary works of Taras Shevchenko, and authored a book about the great writer titled "Shevchenko's Testament". He was also an avid student of the Ukrainian immigration movement in Canada and the United States, collecting historical materials dealing with the movement, and even published a manuscript about his family's roots in Ukraine and later Canada.

Mr. Panchuk donated his substantial personal library of Ukrainian books and other materials to Harvard University, the University of Michigan and the University of Minnesota. He also established a Ukrainian Studies Scholarship Fund at the University of Michigan to promote and encourage younger generations of Ukrainian Americans to specialize in Ukrainian studies.

John Panchuk passed away in 1981 at the age of 77 and was laid to rest in Linden, Michigan by a Ukrainian Orthodox clergyman, Rev. Stolarchuk.

* * * * *

It is regrettable that the vertical development and contributions of the younger generations has to be incomplete. We have not included those who distinguished themselves after 1930: John Machyla, Nicholas Krelaty, John Prohopchuk, John Eliuk, Walter and Tony Wachna, John Dolynchuk and the Cesmustruk boys and Mrs. Anne Ralko. The completion of the list must be left to future writers.

Chapter 4
Living off the Land

When the settlers left Ukraine they were encouraged by Dr. Oleskiw to take their tools and some farm equipment. He had hoped that some artisans could develop their trade and establish an industry. In the Ukraine, weavers, tailors, furriers, potters, blacksmiths, cabinet makers and carpenters made a better living than the peasants who depended on what they earned working for larger land owners, and on what they were able to glean from their small holdings of a few morgens.

The settlers brought their carpenter tools. Some brought sickles, cradles and scythes. Of course the axe and the spade and the hoe were included. These articles were not easy to transport.

When 1897 arrived with axe, spade and hoe they cleared patches of land and planted gardens – the women having brought small bundles of seeds planted them.

Even in the fall of 1896 one or two acquired oxen and could plough small patches of land, and by August 26, 1897 when Leon Roy visited one hundred and forty settlers, he found that they had broken and had in crop the following acreage:

Under wheat	39½
Under oats	24
Under barley	30
Rye	2½
Under vegetables	77

In addition to their crops, he also reported that they had acquired animals:

Milch cows	128
Number of young cattle	
Working oxen and horses	234
Number of poultry	1084[1]

When they settled in Stuartburn, the settlers hope to acquire their farm animals and poultry from the Mennonites in Steinbach. However, the distance, the lack of roads and the swamps and bogs around the Rat River and the Mosquito Creek made it difficult to reach the thriving settlement. On the other hand the Anglo-Saxon and German settlers to the west were closer; the Ukrainian settlers, therefore, were a boon to the more established farmers, as they were able to sell the surplus of their animals. We have the following recorded by one of the settlers:

---

1 Leon Roy to W. F. McCreary, Commissioner of Immigration, Winnipeg (65335)

> We bought cows, oxen and other cattle from our English neighbors but we bought flour and machinery in Dominion City (Our people called it Minitsity). Groceries and other necessities we bought in the local store which is now owned by John Probizansky. This store belonged at that time to a Frenchman called Houle. The stock in his store was not large but it was very handy to be able to acquire some urgent needs. The handiest town for us was Dominion City. It is eighteen miles from the centre established by our settlers. There were incidents when people carried flour on their backs all this distance in order to ensure that their children would not go hungry. The road from Stuartburn to Dominion City was cleared of bush and was fairly adequate. There were some low wet spots, but it was possible to cross them without much difficulty.*

There was better arable land available in the Canadian west – The Northwest Territories and those who chose to live there did not have to toil endlessly on land that was hard to develop.

From the first year in the settlement some men and boys went to work and girls went west to Dominion City and Emerson to work in farm homes. There was a practice, particularly among the earlier German settlers to hire men on a yearly basis. In such homes the women were left to carry on on their own to provide food and bring up a family.

The geography of the area which later formed the greater part of the provincial constituency of Emerson had many minus qualities. Years later, the distinguished Manitoba agronomist, K. S. Prodan summarized the agricultural potential of the area thus:

> The soil in this district is light with patches of black top soil (charozem) and clay. There are also stony patches with granite and limestone predominating. Due to the fact that the area is flat and the banks of the Roseau River, which some also call Rosa, are in places rather low this district has many areas of low lying land, some are rather wet. Vegetables grow here exceptionally well. Potatoes are large and clean. Onions grow to about three inches in diameter. And onion sets grow so well that this district supplies onion sets for seed purposes for all of Western Canada. If Western Canada cannot utilize all the available supply, it is then exported to New York where there is a great need for seed onions. Cucumbers and pumpkins grow well in this area without any additional care in hot-beds and hot houses. Cereal crops, buckwheat, rye, barley, oats and wheat grow well. Fruit can be grown here much better than in other districts where Ukrainians live.**

When the husbands went to work the women took charge of the homestead, planted a garden and provided food and care for the family and having to depend on their own resources, they soon began to reap not what they had planted, but what nature provided. It was the Seneca root.

Seneca Root (Polygala Senega)

Early in the life of the new settlement the pioneers learned about the

---

* F. Voloshyn, Svoboda (USA)

** K. S. Prodan, THE LEADER, Winnipeg, 1931, p. 35

Seneca root plant. It may be that they saw the Indians digging Seneca roots and selling the dried roots which had medicinal potential, and grew in profusion along the ridges. The women found that they could make enough money for their immediate needs by digging these roots. For several years during the early days the women would take their children with them into the areas where the roots grew.

> ...After a day's digging they would have a flour bag full plus an apron full to carry home. This they dried in the sun and sold it at Jack Ramsey's 2 lb.for 25¢ cash. Later when Theo Wachna's had opened a store here, they were able to get 15¢ a lb.when buying groceries or other goods.
>
> Mrs. Gorman (89) April, 1974.

In his book Mr. Peter Humeniuk stated that the "roots" helped to tide over many a settler during periods of financial stress.

Later some people even travelled into the Interlake region to dig roots. It seems, that the root digging areas were badly depleted. Therefore, some women – leaving the small children with older daughters – went south of the 49th parallel to dig for roots in the Indian country. Others drove out by wagon – an organized group – in the Interlake country and dug in the "snake area" around Narcisse. They would not give up.

Marsh Hay

To the east of the Roseau River, and north of the present village of Vita was low lying land inundated each year by the Rat River and the Mosquito Creek that had little potential for agricultural development.

However, the people were alert and found out that the grass that grew in the bogs could be cut and sold to the Americans. This helped them supplement their homestead "income".

In the marshes, there grew a particular kind of grass that was suitable for the making of whitewashing brushes. Here again the women hitched up their skirts and went into the marsh lands to help harvest the wire grass. The problem was the cutting, drying and the bundling of this grass. It was found that it was impossible to harvest this grass using the mower and the hayrake. The muskeg would not hold the weight of the horse and the animals would break through the matted fiber and get mired. The Ukrainian farmers, therefore, re-established the skills and tools employed by their forebearers. They found that they could use the scythe and the sickle, for the cutting of the grass and with the help of a hand rake they rolled the long grass into huge sheaves, bound them and were able to carry these out to higher ground and transport them to Vita.

In the hamlet of Vita the Oshkosh Grass* Company erected huge sheds (which were painted green). The bundles were stored in these sheds and then

* Information provided by W. Kolisnyk

transferred in flat cars to urban centres where long grass was made into brushes.

Often people who study and analyze their work soon discover the means to reduce hard manual labour. It was discovered that if they fashioned boards that looked like short skiis and attached these to the horses' hooves, the horses would be able to walk on the muskeg without breaking through. This invention, consequently, shortened the haying season and reduced toil and made it possible for the people to increase the acreage harvested. Farmers, consequently were able to augment their farm income while the grass grew and there was an adequate demand for brushes.

In time as drainage improved and drier years followed the "grass crop" diminished and this part of the operation became unprofitable.*

Frogs (Rana Papiens)

The marsh lands along the Roseau and the Rat Rivers were good breeding places for mosquitoes. They also provided proper sanctuary for the frogs; during the wet years 1926-28, these marshes and creeks became overpopulated with them. In time these mammals became a nuisance: As night began to fall they started to croak and to leave the water holes and the river and hop out "to explore".

These animals left the bank of the Roseau River and the marsh lands in such numbers that they would be everywhere. When a wagon or a car drove by they would be massacred by the hundred. This made the roads in the hamlet of Gardenton rather unattractive.

> One day some American travellers drove through Gardenton and on seeing all these frogs being mutilated suggested to the people that they catch them and ship them to Minniapolis where they would be processed and prepared for the gourmet tables. Some people got interested (this enterprise became solely a man's endeavour) and shipped the frogs live by train. The first attempt had its problems. Frogs had to be placed in crates with enough water in them to keep them alive. Problems developed: at times the crates would fall as the train shunted and spill out the water. Some crates would break and the frogs would get out. The trainmen then had to catch them and place them in crates again. This was not a pleasant task. It was also discovered that if there was a thunder storm the electrical charges seemed to electrocute the frogs and there was a great loss.

In 1933, Joseph Krelaty, of Gardenton, related how the frog business developed around the Roseau River. Frogs seemed to be everywhere where there was water and people were out to catch them.

Various means were used to catch frogs. Some men waited till after nightfall when the frogs would leave the river or marsh and hop farther away into the higher area. Then the men would make a trench and also place barricades made of burlap. In the morning the frogs would be found behind these barricades as they were unable to jump over them and get into the river.

---

* Information provided by the late William Kolisnyk

They would be scooped into sacks and be taken to the stores to be weighed. At first the storekeepers refused to have anything to do with this trade, but later they paid by the pound live weight. Since only the legs were edible – they were detached because only the legs were bought. Frog's legs sold for about 75¢ a pound. A person could sink a net into an old well and "fish out" $100 worth of frogs. Dealing in frogs became good business and most storekeepers became involved in it. It is claimed that one young man started with very little capital and before long was driving a brand new car. He became a successful "frog buyer". Frog leg export became part of the international trade. After a while stations were established where the frogs would be sold.

> Before long an Illinois company set up a buying station and a processing plant in Dominion City. They hired about half a dozen or so employees locally, and were soon shipping the canned frogs all over the states. Since there were so many frogs around, the supply was both plentiful and profitable. There were also buyers at Stuartburn, Tolstoi, Gardenton and Vita. They would buy most of the frogs from farmers and truck them to Dominion City.* Quite a few farmers never bothered seeding one year: they just chased around the countryside catching frogs.** [1]

Blueberries

And nature still provided another gift to help the settlers earn some money. This gift originally was for the bears, but in time the women, mostly girls, went into the Sandilands "reserve" to pick blueberries that were shipped to Winnipeg.

Picking Blueberries in Sandilands

"My parents took a homestead in the Zhoda area and I grew up there. I went to school until I finished grade four, then I stayed at home and helped to clear the land.

One late summer when I was in my teens, my father took me along with about ten other girls in the neighborhood to pick blueberries in the Sandilands Reserve. We not only brought receptacles for the berries, but also food, a change of clothing and some bedding. My father left us in an old camp where we could sleep on the floor. We did our cooking outside and took the berries to a store in Sandilands where we received 25¢ for a two pound pail.

Picking blueberries among the rocks and the bushes was hard. It was hot, too. To protect us from getting a sunstroke, we used to place a large burdock leaf on top of our head. It was held in place with our kerchief.

When the weekend would arrive, we would see my father drive to the camp to replenish our food supply, and I would give him the money I earned from the sale of the berries I picked. The next day we would go into the bush

---

* It appears that this was the end of Dominion City business being able to profit from the efforts and enterprise of their neighbours to the east.

** J. M. Waddell, Dominion City Facts, Fiction and Hyperbole, 1970, p.46.

1 Now it is illegal to catch frogs.

again. To find better blueberry areas, at times, we wandered as far as eight miles from the camp. We each had large pails with us to carry the berries to our camp and would tie the pails to each end of a pole to form a crude yoke and then we would wend our way among the rocks being careful not to fall and spill the day's picking. Now when I watch T.V. and see Chinese men and women carrying their produce to the market on a pole slung over the shoulders, it reminds me of the Sandilands blueberries.

Our worst problem was with water. The water we would bring with us would soon get warm, and one wanted a cold drink to get refreshed from the heat. The rocks were hot and when heated by the sun they would retain the heat for a long time and we could not dig water holes close to them. The only way we could get a cool drink was to dig a hole in the muskeg and the water would come up cool and fresh, but not too clear, so we had to strain it through a kerchief or a piece of cloth.

This year I have been married for 60 years (1980) and whenever I bake a blueberry pie, I recall the Sandilands blueberries. I can see the gaunt figures of young girls, suntanned, scratched by the bushes and mosquito bitten – I couldn't see myself but I looked as they did wearing a kerchief and having blueberry stained hands. 'Oj, tak, tak...', Oh, that's the way it was."

The supplementary products that helped the homesteaders survive soon became depleted or disappeared. The dairy aspect, however, continued and cattle raising began to provide a good source of farm income. However, as improvements were made and drainage improved, marsh hay and frog business came to an end; the attempts to grow wild rice saw an abortive end also.

Improved drainage, one year caught the farmers short of hay and they had to move their stock east to be able to winter them. Adjustments had to be made.

The Tolstoi area depended more on grain farming and a grain elevator was built in the hamlet. The growing of buckwheat saw a few years of success also.

C. S. Prodan's leadership (continued by John Negrych) in introducing better poultry, sheep, swine and also pre-bred cattle brought better days to the area. Consequently, larger cattle herds were established, pasturage area had to increase. and the number of farmers per section decreased.

In the Zhoda area, availability of heavy equipment and use of fertilizer made a change. The peatmoss was burned-off and stones were pushed into large piles and cereal grains were planted. Things did change. The land that one writer described as being one that could break the back and heart of the stoutest man, did not crush the Ukrainian farmer. And they made progress. During the pre-WWII period "The Free Press Prairie Farmer" made the following report on the Vita area:

> So little grain is shipped from the district around Vita in southeastern Manitoba that there is no elevator in that busy little town. The Ukrainian farmers there are making a living form products other than wheat.

The soil is light but they are making good use of their resources. Grass crops hold down the soil and this year over 300 farmers in that territory seeded 10,000 pounds of brome, alfalfa and crested wheat grass, the agricultural representative of the Manitoba government, J. Negrych, reported.

Sheep are increasing. A survey through the schools in the neighboring country this spring showed that 364 farmers had 7,740 sheep. This gives an average of 21 ewes and their lambs per farm keeping sheep, but most of the flocks were smaller. Five of the larger sheepmen had an average of 90 head. Lambs that brought $6 to $6.50 per 100 pounds five years ago are now bringing $11 to $12. Wool that brought five cents a pound in 1936 now sells at 26 cents.

Honey is chiefly sold locally. It used to bring 60 cents for a 10-pound pail, now 90 cents to $1.00. Not much garden stuff is sold from the district except potatoes toward spring.

They are improving the equality of their poultry. They bought through poultry clubs last year, 4,000 chicks, this year 13,000. They sell their fattened cockerels to a Winnipeg department store and can get about $1.25 per bird. The young male birds bring 23 cents a pound and the fowls that have finished their usefulness as layers sell at 16 cents. The fowls are better value for the money, the agriculture representative remarked.

But the main source of income is the cream cheque. In the first six months of last year the Vita creamery took in 141,000 pounds of butterfat, this year 186,000 pounds. The new bonus that will take the table cream price form 32 cents to 38 cents should further speed up production.

Fig. 1 Women at work.

Part V
Life as Canadian Citizens

Chapter 1

Written Records and Cultural Advancement

There was not an overabundance of people in the creative field among the Ukrainian settlements east of the Red River. The first, as can be determined, was Wasyl Kudryk. He was a qualified teacher from the village of Cebriv in Ukraine. He acquired a teaching certificate in Manitoba and taught in several school district.

During his life time he wrote copiously, but much of his writing was of the religious polemics category. However, he had great creative ability, writing poetry and had he devoted time to fiction; he could have produced a Canadian classic like Maria Chaptelaine. He wrote some credible poetry and his early essays and short stories had some tinge of mysticism and romanticism.

Wasyl Kudryk, regrettably wrote in Ukrainian only and left no record in English. Besides writing creatively, he was engaged in journalism and was editor of a Ukrainian paper, "Ukrainian Voice".

Peter Humeniuk

Following in the footsteps of Wasyl Kudryk was a brilliant teacher, Peter Humeniuk, who grew up on his father's farm south of Stuartburn. On retirement he wrote in a Ukrainian paper, "The Canadian Farmer" a longer series of articles about life in the settlement where he grew up and later on the suggestion of his friend and former pupil, rewrote the material in English and published a fine book, Hardships and Progress of Ukrainian Pioneers.[1]

Emanating from the same area was a biographical book, Son of Pioneers by Felix Tsesarski one of Mr. Peter Humeniuk's pupils in Tolstoi school, who became a school teacher and then an insurance agent.

Then Joseph Kohut's reminiscences appeared in print dealing with the organization of the Stuartburn Ukrainian Catholic church and the description of the village of Senkiw from which many of the first settlers came. The publication of Vita: A Ukrainian Community by Michael Ewanchuk[2] and Look Who's Coming: The Wachna Story add to the written records about the first Ukrainian settlement in Manitoba.

Nevertheless, people like C. S. Prodan also recorded much valuable information about the pioneer settlers in the area southeast of Dominion City.

In 1971 John Panchuk published a valuable brochure in Battle Creek, Michigan. This Canadian exile prepared a well-researched study titled "Bukovynian Settlements in Southern Manitoba (Gardenton Area)". It is a

1 Peter Humeniuk – Hardships and Progress of Ukrainian Pioneers, Peter Humeniuk publisher, Derksen Printers, Steinbach MB, 1977, 236 pp.
2 M. Ewanchuk, Vita a Ukrainian Community, Derksen Printers, Steinbach, MB, 1979.

well-illustrated and a well-documented 86 page brochure that contains much historical information about the early Ukrainian settlers from the Ukrainian province of Bukovyna.

In 1979 a memorial book marking the celebration of the 60th anniversary of the Ukrainian National Home in Vita appeared in print in Ukrainian language. It carries a fairly detailed list of names of people associated with the organization.

Michael Stashyn who came with 1896 group as a child, wrote his reminiscences in the "Ukrainian Voice". These constitute a valuable source of information for future readers and writers.

And, in conclusion, it must be emphasized that much valuable information about the area may be gleaned from letters to the editor in various Ukrainian newspapers. And it must be stated that the collection and interpretation the articles are receiving awaits future writers. At the present time Prof. J. C. Lehr of the University of Winnipeg is carrying out a detailed research about the area.

Cultural Advancement

From the start the settlement began to make progress, not only in developing the farms, and in the organization of schools, but also in some people going into business. The organization of parishes and building of churches was an activity that commenced early in the life of the settlement. This called for the homesteaders to meet and plan together. They met in homes since other accommodation was not available.

A Desire of Settlers to Maintain Contact

There was a great desire on the part of the settlers who arrived to form the Oleskiw settlement in the Stuartburn area in 1896 to establish an organization like the "Prosvita" with its library facilities they left in Ukraine. It was in these organizational centres that they first had an opportunity to read Dr. Oleskiw's bulletins about "Free Lands" what led them to leave their native land. In Canada they tried to organize themselves into similar groups.

It must be stressed again that in spite of a few gatherings, the homesteaders experienced extreme isolation as they took up land to the east of Stuartburn – the women more so than the men. Men went to work and had an opportunity to come in contact with other people and to observe the progress made by other communities – people who preceded them as settlers to Canada by ten years or more.

The building of homes was the first opportunity for people to meet in larger numbers. Here was an opportunity for them to assemble and help out each other. They met at bees, mostly bees for the daubing of a new home with mud plaster. Often this project was followed by a social event – a dinner and, at times, even a dance.

True, people met when they went to shop: first in Dominion City and later in local stores where they started to trade and receive their mail.

The rural schools soon provided some opportunity to hold meetings or hear lectures. This started during elections when representatives of political parties and candidates came to present their programmes. The people, however, craved cultural centres. They were disenchanted that with the late organization of schools, their children were deprived of exposure to culture – Ukrainian and Canadian – as a consequence, some were growing up illiterate in the "land of promise".

One significant event that provided impetus to the building of community centres was the moving of the municipal hall of the R.M. of Stuartburn from Stuartburn to Vita. The primary objective of this move was not only to have the office more centrally located, but at the same time to remove it from the excessive Anglo-Saxon sphere of influence.

After 1906 rural school teachers arrived in the area. The holding of a Christmas concert in the school house was a significant event to provide the parents with a degree of rejoicing and enriched the life of the children.

The municipal hall in Vita offered a new place to meet. Not only that, but under the leadership of the local teacher, and the assistance of local leaders, it was possible to organize an amateur club of young people and stage a play. Other activities followed: a library was organized. This library was a great boon to the settlers; some older people wanting to use the library even made an effort to learn to read and succeeded. As a consequence, in time, the Vita community became one of the more culturally enlightened Ukrainian communities in Manitoba. Fortunately, later Vita had a Mr. D. Ukryniuk who was able to develop music; through the years he trained good choirs.

Communication with Outside World

Communication with Ukraine and Ukrainians in other parts of the world was through the Ukrainian newspapers. At the start an odd one received a newspaper from Ukraine, then the American newspaper "Svoboda" whose one-time editor was Rev. Nestor Dmytriw. In 1903 the first Ukrainian paper published in Canada was subscribed to. It was the "Canadian Farmer", followed in 1910 by the Winnipeg published periodical, "Ukrainian Voice" which became popular because a one-time Tolstoi resident, Wasyl Kudryk, was its editor. The Ukrainian Catholics published "The Canadian Ukrainian". These three newspapers for years influenced the whole community.

There were radical papers published in Canada, too, "The Labouring People" and News (Novyny) in Edmonton, but subscription of these papers was negligible. The Canadian Morning" of the Presbyterian church did not make any inroads either. For a while a "Ruski"-oriented newspaper edited by a russified priest, Bozyk did not gain any popularity in the orthodox sector south-east of the hamlet of Gardenton.

Great credit is due to the people and clergy in the area for creating a climate that saw the coming into being of fine women's organizations that helped improve the life of the women and enrich the life of the community.

The organized life of the people followed the same pattern as in Stuartburn, Tolstoi, Rosa, Sarto, Vita and Gardenton. Interestingly enough the Arbakka area actually showed very early organizational development. It is significant to note that organizational life in community centres flourished more where there were capable teachers to assume leadership.

The building of community centres provided an opportunity for young people to meet. Hence house parties were discontinued and dances were held in community centres where there was good adult supervision and the use of alcoholic beverages was forbidden.

As moving picture machines became available the community halls also became a place for "picture shows".

Fig. 1 Peter Humeniuk

Chapter 2

Community Leaders

The first leader of the Oleskiw settlers, of course, was Cyril Genik, but he did not remain long in the area. Nevertheless, even from Winnipeg, where he established residence in 1897, he made himself available when called upon.

Rev. Nestor Dmytriw during his two visits encouraged the settlers and gave them guidance and suggested ways they could get better established.

Theodosy Wachna

In 1897, however, there arrived a man in the area who, after leaving the Ukraine went to live in the U.S.A., where he worked as a miner and attended night school to learn English. After a few years there he read the advertisement of the Canadian government about opportunities that awaited settlers in the Canadian prairies. Consequently, he left for Winnipeg where the immigration official engaged him to lead a group of settlers into the Stuartburn area. He arrived in the hamlet of Stuartburn and remained there all his life.

Soon after his arrival, he married a local girl, Anna Prygroski, and they settled on the farm. However, he did not stay farming but got involved in various activities and became the first leader among the new settlers. During his lifetime in the district he was a farmer, an immigration agent, a postmaster, a secretary-treasurer of a Municipality, a Justice of the Peace, a notary public and a merchant. He operated a store in Stuartburn and later in Gardenton. Theodosy Wachna was a busy man.

It is important to observe that he laid great stress on education and his fifteen children made good progress. Elias was the first one to become a professional man, a dentist. Tony was a doctor, several became teachers and others went into business. It is remarkable that he not only succeeded as a father of a large family, but he was one of the few pioneers in the area who did exceptionally well financially. Through the years he received fine support from his wife, Anna.*

C. S. Prodan

Among the personalities that merit recognition for the leadership provided to help develop the Vita community, the name of C. S. Prodan leads the list. His selfless attitude and genuine effort to bring about improvements reduced the number who were on the verge of leaving their unprofitable farms and made life tolerable for those who remained.

C. S. Prodan started his career as a school teacher. His life in rural Manitoba gave him insight and understanding of the needs of the Manitoba farmers, and Ukrainian farmers in particular, who settled in Manitoba at the

* Vidi: 60th Anniversary of Theodosy and Anna Wachna, 1957.

time when the better lands were too costly and to acquire a homestead they were placed on less productive and submarginal land. Mr. Prodan studied agriculture at the Manitoba Agricultural College and received employment with the Manitoba Department of Agriculture as field representative. His assignment was mainly among farmers of Ukrainian extraction.

The Manitoba Department of Agriculture in its wisdom permitted him to use the Ukrainian language in his lectures as some people lacked adequate knowledge of the English language to understand some of the technical vocabulary needed to explain agricultural processes.

Mr. Prodan, in addition to other areas, devoted a great amount of time to the Vita area. In his lectures and when he held agricultural short courses of two or three day duration, he utilized charts and diagrams to explain concepts and utilized a battery operated movie projector. The movie projector served to develop higher interest and to make his lectures more comprehensible. His lectures were given in rural school houses and in the National Homes in the area. He maintained close contacts with rural school teachers, many his friends, who accommodated him in their humble teacherages.

The residents of the Vita area credit him with the improvements of living conditions in the area by helping to make the farms more productive.

He helped to develop better approaches to poultry raising and introduced new strains. Better dressing of poultry and marketing of turkeys brought in added revenue to the district. In the dairy field there was a marked improvement in the selection of milch cows. Milk samples were tested and suggestions were made for the elimination of poor milkers. Vegetable growing was also modified.

He introduced the growing of onions; the soil was light and onion growing became a success. Vita onion sets were leading the sales in Canada, and even the U.S.A. Overproduction, however, put an end to onion growing.

Sheep raising was introduced and he used to cart around a pure bred ram to improve the stock. His successor, John Negrych did the same. C. S. Prodan did much to improve the lot of his fellow men.

Mr. Prodan, not only carried his duties out in the most energetic manner, he also was interested in the history of the area and collected much of the early history of the settlement.

Since it is impossible in this study, to give all those who did act as leaders; however, we shall deal in greater detail only with three men who started in the area as young men and subsequently provided leadership.

Nazar Bodnarchuk

There were several brothers in the Bodnarchuk family. Michael stayed in the Shevchenko area from the start. And one went to Alberta, one to Windsor ON, and Oleksa farmed in Roseilsle, MB and then became a barber in Rathwell. Nazar went working as a railway worker and became a section foreman. He married an East Selkirk girl and they raised a fine large family. When the Vita people organized a Co-op store he left the track work to manage it. In time he owned the business, later becoming an operator of Vita Hotel.

Two of his daughters married professional men, one William Prochuk, and Helen married an engineer, Michael Lasko. Their sons are in the professions.

Nazar Bodnarchuk was a capable man. It was claimed that he was the best read man in Vita. His contribution to the community was positive.

He took an active part in politics. Since J. Kulachkowsky was a Tory he was a strong Grit. He was interested in education and on retirement established a scholarship at St. Andrews College.

Dmytro Ukryniuk

Started farming in Broad Valley, MB, then took a dairy course and when the Crescent Creamery opened a creamery in Vita, he became its first manager. Vita was a good centre for a creamery and the cream cheques helped the farmers manage even through the hard years.

Mr. Ukryniuk's additional contribution to the community was in music. He conducted a choir in the National Home and also led a good choir in the Orthodox church. Mrs. Ukryniuk participated in community affairs. They raised a boy and three girls; Olga was a teacher, one lives in the eastern states - and Halia, Mrs. Symchych, in Minneapolis. The son passed away early in life.

With his musical ability he contributed much to the quality of life in the area and Vita community staged many fine plays and concerts.

During the thirties Mr. Ukryniuk and his choir travelled to the neighboring districts giving concerts to collect funds for the Vita Hospital.

After he built his own creamery in Tolstoi, he gave up the management of the Crescent Creamery in Vita. Later he operated a creamery in Gilbert Plains and Winnipeg and was successful in his ventures.

Joseph Kulachkowsky

It seems that the early leaders in the community were men engaged in business and in the Vita area it was a school teacher who went into business. Here is part of his record:

> I, Joseph Kulachkowsky, the son of John and Antonia nee Lewetsky, of the village of Senkiw, district of Zalischyky in Western Ukraine was born March 15, 1887. I came to Canada with my parents to settle in Stuartburn, Manitoba. My parents settled on a farm two miles south from the hamlet. During the summer I helped my father on the farm and attended Stuartburn school during the winter months.
>
> In 1904 I went to the Ukrainian Training school (in Minto) where I stayed during the school years 1904, 05 and 06. On December 22, 1906 I received a teacher's diploma. In January 1907, I started to teach in the Shevchenko school at $410.00

per annum and stayed there for two years.

In 1909 I married Lena Saranchuk and went to teach in Arbakka. As there was no living accommodation, with the help of local farmers I built a teacherage.

I taught there for two years and then:

- March 1911, appointed Notary Public
- In 1912 I was a tax collector for the Bank of Ottawa at Emerson and also for the Dominion Trust Co. in Winnipeg
- April 1913 received appointment as Postmaster and the Post Office was lo cated in our store, with my wife really being the postmistress.
- I joined the Conservative party and like John Probizansky was a Conservative party organizer and looked after road building.*

We raised three girls and two boys. Helen and Mary became teachers, Olesia a postmistress, one boy went to the U.S.A. and the other was in business in Dominion City.

John Probizansky

One of the better known community leaders of Stuartburn was John Probizansky. He was a hard-working man who seemed to have a capacity to succeed in his endeavors. He operated a store in Stuartburn where his family residence was attached to the store and in the upstairs part there was accommodation for travellers. Since there was no hotel in the hamlet, the travellers who were driven around by Frank Miller used to stop over at the Probizanskys. He was an active member in the community and a good leader, serving as trustee and a director of the local community centre, the Narodny Dim. He was judicious in his actions, but kind and humble and willing to help those in need.

During my thirty-five years in Canada, I have been a farmer, a road inspector, a storekeeper, a postmaster and a good conservative. I came to the New Country, Canada, in 1896. I was only sixteen years old then and settled in the Stuartburn area. My father, Mateij and my mother followed me.

I settled on a farm SW 23-2-6 four miles east of Stuartburn and in 1899 I married Catherine Bednar. We raised 10 children. When we lived on the farm, I took an active part in organizing the Ukrainian Catholic church and the Svoboda (Beckett) school district. In the early days the trail between Stuartburn and Vita ran through our farm and we were always in touch with the people. In time Mr. Theodosy Wachna established a larger store in Gardenton (New Stuartburn) and I started as a storekeeper in Old Stuartburn, after having farmed for 25 years.
Things are beginning to improve here now: the new claydump will soon be a good highway to Vita, but one still gets stuck in the gumbo flats on the way to Dominion City. But this will change, too, if the government allots more money for road building.

---

* From J. Kulachkowsky records. Courtesy Mrs. Olesia Smook.

The popularity of the Probizanskys may be judged by the large number of people who attended their Golden Wedding anniversary. We notice names like Ramsey, Johnson and Remus: after fifty years, there was unity where once there was diversity.

> Out of town guests attending their celebration included: J. R. Solomon, M.L.A., Rev. Dr. Kushnir, Mr. Yaremowich, Mr. and Mrs. Bill Kosowan, Mr. and Mrs. H. Bugera. Mr. and Mrs. E. Cassian. Mr. and Mrs. H. Zuk. Rev. Chenichi. John Zuk, Mr. John Goy, all of Winnipeg.
>
> Dominion City guests were Mr. And Mrs. Alton Johnson, Mr. R. Ramsey, Mr. M. Sokolick. Mr. and Mrs. Paley. Others were Mr. and Mrs. Nestor Kostynuik of Windsor, Ont. Mr. and Mrs. M. Fosty and Mr. and Mrs. Kohut of Ridgeville, Mr. and Mrs. W. Remus of Emerson, Mr. Wm. Rekunyk and Mr. and Mrs. Bill Kohut of Toronto, Ont. Also guests from Vita, Gardenton, Tolstoi, Woodmore, Sarto and Sundown were present.

Besides farming and later being in business – John Probizansky was an active community member. He was a treasurer of the Ukrainian Catholic church for most of his days. He helped organize a co-op store in Vita, and became resident of the Vita co-operative creamery. He always tried to help in the community and during WWII when farm help was difficult to get, he went out to help with the harvest. Wrote Marjorie Stevens in her press report: "He's still out there pitching."

The first three were early leaders who were followed later by others no less capable, and who made a fine input to enrich the cultural life of the community.

Gardenton

After the railway line went east from Emerson, Theo Wachna came into business there while Mrs. Wachna continued in Stuartburn. There was a flour mill in the hamlet and a Mr. Kossowan, a school teacher, built a hotel. Two others, Mr. Sidorski and Mr. Krelaty, were two storekeepers, later Mr. Onysko; and with them rested Gardenton leadership.

Arbakka (a name of Icelandic origin, the bank of a river)

Mr. W. Jerowsky, one of the teachers of the first group, taught in Arbakka for many years and his wife also operated a store. Mr. N. Eliuk was a successful farmer and ran a store. The two men provided the leadership in the small community just north of the 49th parallel. Most of the children of Mr. and Mrs. Eliuk got a high school education, some, like John, became teachers.

Caliento

This was a small centre with a fine Greek Catholic church. There a teacher of Mr. Jerowsky's vintage, Mr. Maliniuk, was in business with

Wasylyshyn; Wlasiuk was in business, too. In time a centre opened up in Sundown and Zhoda had a post office.

Nicholas Dolynchuk of Tolstoi – A Success Story

The area west of Tolstoi had better land and was a better business centre. Mr. N. Dolynchuk ran a successful business for many years and was capably assisted by his wife.

Nicholas Dolynchuk was only 16 years of age when he landed in Montreal in 1904, and stayed working in a steel mill. However, he wanted to go west to be with his brother Simon who had a homestead in Caliento. From Caliento he moved to Tolstoi where at 21 he met and married Irene Melinik whose parents arrived in the Tolstoi area in 1897. Nicholas was from the selo of Warwaryntsi. The Meliniks were part of the early Oleskiw settlers. In spite of the fact that Irene did not have an opportunity to attend school in Canada, and neither did Nicholas though he did in the Ukraine, they went into business and spent 26 very successful years in Tolstoi.

The Dolynchuks raised three boys, John, Alexander, Nestor and one daughter Mary Hrynyk. His sons operated a meat market in Winnipeg where the Dolynchuks retired to continue active membership in the Ukrainian Orthodox church. Their son John married a school teacher Olga Popiel and their daughter Helen became Dr. Ihor Mayba's bride. Their great grandson is a successful physician in Winnipeg and Dr. John Mayba has also distinguished himself as a very capable church choir director.

Mr. Kostynuk, Mr. Fosty, Mandzj, Yarinie and W. Kolodzinski were in business, too. Mr. Kolodzinski was a grain buyer as there was a grain elevator in the village. The village had two or three churches and a good National Home. Miss Maria Yarinie was an active member of an amateur club. She married Rev. Frank Kernitsky.

Fig. 1 Ukrainian National Home, Tolstoi, Manitoba

Senkiw – Rosa – Sarto

North of Stuartburn were these small centres with small stores and post offices. A Hnat Iwonczuk moved into the area from south of Gardenton. He distinguished himself by helping his son, Theodore, graduate as a doctor. In Sarto, Mr. Nykoforuk who was said to have had a good library helped with the development of an amateur club. The programmes in the National Home helped to enhance the cultural and recreational life of the district.

In Rosa two men were in the lead: Mr. Peter Tanchak and Mr. Paley.

A successful school teacher, Isidore Goresky, who left for the province for Alberta, rates Mr. Paley as a good leader who though lost his investment, recouped as a farmer in the Dominion City area. Mr. Goresky married Anna, John Paley's daughter. In his memoirs, Isidore Goresky notes that Peter Tanchak and N. Paley were both capable men and in politics, etc. were generally juxtaposed.

Peter Tanchak

One of the more progressive and capable men in the Rosa area was Peter Tanchak. Though many of the settlers in the district were Ukrainian Catholic, he belonged to the Orthodox group and was connected by marriage to the Mihaychuks in Arbakka. Mrs. Tanchak was also a capable woman and took the lead in organizing a women's organization that did much to improve the quality of life of the settlers in the district. The Tanchaks were good farmers and they also kept a small store to augment their income.

Though Rosa was not close to any high school in the district, the Tanchaks raised five boys and one girl, Bill, John, Dmytro, Manuel, Stephen and Helen, and all received their high school education and became teachers. John was a capable teacher and when Mr. J. R. Solomon was appointed to the Bench, John was elected in his place.

Misfortune took away Peter Tanchak at an early age: He was killed in a car accident in Morris MB.

Mr. Michael Kadyniuk who was a Zhoda teacher moved to Vita to become Secretary-treasurer of the Municipality and served the people well. Mr. Mysak also made a contribution. During the formative years the Podolskis ran a successful business.

The Vita Community Hall, Narodnyj Dim was the community centre, leadership was local. During the early years there was no principals of Ukrainian extraction to take an active community role.

The Vita hamlet received good support from the farmers.

Dr. Harold Waldon

Another man who contributed immeasurably to the improvement of life in the Vita area was a Killarney-born doctor, Harold Waldon. True the

Ukrainians who came to Canada in 1896 and after were healthy people; this may be judged from the figures of immigrants arriving in Canada: Only 11 Ukrainians and 10 Poles were detained in Montreal hospital and 21 of each of these two groups were detained for trachoma; on the other hand, Italians, Russians and Syrians were most affected with trachoma. Some immigrants had to be deported for health reasons. Governmental figures show the following deportations: Icelanders, 1:224; Hebrews, 1:336; Poles, 1:556 and Ukrainians, 1:132.

However, the new settlers of the Vita-Stuartburn area had no easy access to medical services; it was Dominion City or Emerson, or after the railway line was extended to Winnipeg. The people of the Arbakka area, it seems, did get some medical help in Minnesota – in Lancaster and some other hamlets to the south. Nevertheless, in Canada, health problems came early. Mrs. Anna Sirman provided this information:

> A girl died after we arrived and was buried in the first cemetery organized – now abandoned. She died during the smallpox epidemic and our home was quarantined for six weeks – we could not see anybody. People brought us what we needed from the store and left it outside and later we went outside and brought the things into the house.[1]

It was difficult to vaccinate children in the settlement and even in the thirties one could see some school children south of Gardenton who were "pox" marked.

It was fortunate for the people, however, that after W.W.I. a well-to-do lady from Pilot Mound, in memory of the boys lost during the war, it seems, donated a sum of some eighty thousand dollars and a Presbyterian missionary hospital was built in Vita. And it was most fortunate that Dr. Harold Waldon, a war veteran, came to take charge of the hospital. It was a great boon to the

Fig. 2 Dr. Harold Waldon, Dr. Waldon's snowmobile bought by Dmytro Tanchak.

community. Dr. Waldon did not spare himself and worked like a beaver to improve the health of the community. First he travelled by horse and cutter, later using a snowmobile and still later a bombardier.

Fig. 3 Uhryniuk creamery manager talking to a farmer.

Fig. 4 Vita leaders with Prof. Bakerskyj.

Fig. 5 Arbakka people held a meeting beside teacherage 1910.

Chapter 3

Politics

For years there was an effort to elect a Member of the Legislative Assembly from the area particularly one of Ukrainian extraction, but the people could not succeed in nominating one as the conventions of both old parties appeared to be fairly well "rigged".

Early in the life of the settlers east of the Red, there was an attempt to run a candidate of Ukrainian extraction in the Selkirk constituency which included parts of the area east of the Red River. One Wasyl Holowatski, a radical, ran as a Social Democrat (a precursor of the N.D.P.) He, however, did not succeed - by 1911 the Ukrainians were fairly well divided into two camps: Liberal and Conservative.

Professor J. C. Lehr summarizes the situation by pointing out that while at the start the Torries were strongly opposed to the Ukrainian settlers, calling them Clifford Sifton protegees and developing an antagonism towards them inspite of the fact that the editor of the Free Press, John W. Defoe, praised the Ukrainian settlers for the contribution they were making to the development of western Canada. However, noting the large numbers of Ukrainian names on the electors rolls, in about 1903, the Torries made an about face: under the leadership of their provincial leader, R. P. Roblin they began to appoint organizers to promote their party, be it only to an important position of a weed inspector. Nevertheless, some were made organizers of public works projects. Regrettably they built few roads or drained many swamps. Two organizers somehow escaped incarceration - what was really due them. Consequently the people suffered.

Election of the First M.L.A. - D. Yakimischak.

Profitting from the political action of the Ukrainians in the Interlake area who, in 1915, failed to nominate T. D. Ferley as a Liberal candidate (the weed inspectors carried a propaganda to have the Ukrainian delegates vote against him. They were Torry workers). T. D. Ferley, therefore, ran as an Independent and was elected. In 1920 the Ukrainian electors sponsored a lawyer, D. Yakimischak, as an Independent candidate and he was elected and re-elected in 1922. The trouble in the Emerson constituency was that there were two political aspirants, W. Kolodzinski and Joseph Kulachkowsky. In 1926

J. Kulachkowsky ran as a Conservative, split the vote and a Mr. Curran, a Progressive was elected. Other attempts to nominate or elect a candidate of Ukrainian extraction proved unsuccessful.

J. R. Solomon

In 1941, however, John Solomon was elected to represent Emerson as a member of the Liberal Progressive party. He served the people well and did initiate some drainage projects. He was Deputy Speaker of the Legislature, appointed County Court Judge, and in 1971 became Justice of the Court of Queens Bench.

John Tanchak

Succeeding John Solomon was John Tanchak. He was the first representative who was born in the Constituency of Emerson and grew up in the Rosa district. He was well acquainted with the needs of the area having taught high school grades in the Purple Bank school and later became a leading turkey farmer in Manitoba. His farm was located in Ridgeville. Mr. Tanchak also provided leadership in recognizing the contributions of the Ukrainian pioneers in the area and participated in unveiling the monument erected to them in Vita, Manitoba.

Mark Smerchanski M.P.

In 1968 Mark Smerchanski who served in the Legislature as Liberal representative from Burrows, was nominated and elected Liberal Member of Parliament for the Federal Constituency of Provencher. He was a capable representative, but went down to defeat when the Conservative party gained popularity and the Mennonite sector in the constituency became interested in politics and elected a representative of their group. This was the beginning of the Mennonite political ascendancy in the area as their numbers increased and the population of Ukrainians decreased due to outmigration, it seems.

Steven Derewianchuk M.L.A.

In the 1975 election an M.L.A. of the N.D.P. party was elected. He served until 1977 and that seems to be the end of Ukrainian dominance in the Constituency of Emerson as the constituency boundaries were changed.

Chapter 4

Outmigration

During the first eight-year period after the first Ukrainian settlement was formed in Manitoba, outmigration commenced. However, this outmigration was within Canada. Statistics Canada verify this:

Table 1 **Arriving in Canada**

	1903	1904
Ukrainians	10,139	8,247
Poles	279	669

Leaving Canada for the U.S.A. during 1903-04: Ukrainians 07, Poles 62 and Russians 1713.

As far as the number of Ukrainians coming to Canada, we observe a decrease from 10,139 to 8,247. The drop of over 11 percent in immigration for the two years was due - as Cyril Genik observed – to the fact that as numbers leaving Ukraine increased more land became available for sale. A decline in property values ensued, and many who had plans to leave for Canada could not sell their holdings, and acquire the requisite funds for the transplantation of their families to Canada.

Nevertheless, it was Peter Majkowsky of whom Rev. Nestor Dmytriw spoke highly, - and who had the qualities of leadership - who after building a house and acquiring some stock finally made a volte face, saying: "a plague on all the mosquitoes, swamps and stones" and returned to the Ukraine. Others like Maxym Stashyn and Yaremovich left for the North West Territories and did well on farms north of Saskatoon.

The Land Could Not Sustain Many

The Boychuk family came to Canada in 1905 when their daughter, Sophie, was a year old. She grew up in Sundown where the family settled, and married Fedor Olynyk. They farmed in Sundown until 1942 when they moved to Winnipeg, but returned to Sundown in 1969.

It is surprising how the members of the family related to Sophie scattered to various places in Canada and the U.S.A. Of her four daughters, two lived in Winnipeg, Maria Dullevich in Tuscon, Arizona and Alice in Flint, Michigan. Of her three sons, John remained in Sundown, Michael went to Winnipeg and Joe to Fort Frances. Her stepsons: Bill moved to Las Vegas, and Don to McBride, B.C. There was not enough good land in Sundown to sustain many and not enough employment in Manitoba to absorb more of the second generation.

The Boychuk-Olynyk group sets a pattern for hundreds of others of the Stuartburn settlement who spread far and wide.

The Bodnarchuk family that settled in Vita also spread in various parts of the country.

If a close study were made of the pattern of change to gain employment, one would find that to start with the members of the Stuartburn group tended to go to Chicago, Detroit and Windsor, and even closer by to Fort Frances.

And, in summary, the land of the settlement was not fertile enough to make smaller farms economically viable. However, due to the fact that the land was swampy and stony it gave the venturesome a chance to acquire more land at a lower price to go into cattle raising and they succeeded.

There were a few who disregarded the 49th (the border) and settled on land south of Arbakka and even built their church there. A small number bought farms south of Emerson.

A large Tkachyk family took homesteads southwest of Gardenton and in time the younger generation left for points in the U.S.A. and other places in Manitoba.

W. Didkowski who came during the post W.W. I era started farming in Overstone, then Dominion City, but unable to buy a farm there went to Snowflake, MB.

> I went to Snowflake and we bought a farm on "mile one" – north of the U.S.A.-Canadian boundary. We engaged in farming there until we retired and moved to Winnipeg. By that time we owned eleven quarters and operated our farming establishment with modern equipment. Two of my sons farm there on adjacent farms. My other two boys and the four girls did not stay in the district.
>
> Moving into the Snowflake area was not easy. We were going to be the only ones of Ukrainian extraction in the area; and we feared we may be isolated. However, we soon established contact with other Ukrainians in the southern part of Manitoba. Though our Ukrainian neighbors were as far as sixty miles away, we managed to maintain contact and the Pawichs, Kuziws, Trehuks and others, and used to meet with us. The John Nowosads were in Holmfield and John would bring his fiddle and cymbalons along – he was a good musician – and we would have a nice get-together about once a year or so.
>
> We, however, had to live as good members of our Snowflake community. We did partake in events that took place in our neighborhood; and one could not ask for finer people – they made us feel that we belonged. There was no early Red River Valley attitude there; and we lived very happily, inter-visited and phoned each other often.
>
> Though we were not in close contact with any Ukrainian community, we tried to maintain our language and there was one thing my wife and I did: we taught our children to speak and read Ukrainian and gave them some appreciation of the Ukrainian culture and history. Not all of our children, however, married spouses of Ukrainian extraction, but we had no right to expect that. They are all doing well.
>
> Mother and I adjusted well to Winnipeg and we are active members of our Cathedral. We enjoy life here and Canada to us is heaven on earth.*

Very often when settlers left the Ukrainian settlements east of Domin-

---

* Paul Didkowski. Interviewed in Winnipeg.

ion City, they went in groups.

In his memoirs, Isidore Goresky who once lived in southeastern Alberta mentions about the Ukrainians coming there:

> A group of settlers who came from the Stuartburn district in Manitoba to file on homesteads at Hemaraka. The names were those of Sirman, Pidhirny and Senkiw. There were many more at one time, but they had left the area chiefly during the period of drought and settled in the north. Some of them like Zaporzan and Smook settled near Vegreville where they became successful farmers. In 1926 Zaporzan was already experimenting with the growing of fruits on his farm...[1]

Four Zahara families moved in the Peace River country.

The Sarto area close to St. Malo and the Mennonite colony did not give the younger generation a chance to acquire homesteads, consequently, Zinkowski and Hryhirchuk moved to the district northeast of Arborg where they acquired homesteads. Mr. Zinkowski did well and became a Postmaster of Ledwyn P.O.

N. Prygnocki moved to Fisher Branch where he did well as a merchant.

The descendants of Iwan Machnee of Gardenton re-established themselves in the western provinces as farmers.

Dufrost Disrict Established

It appears that Hryc Bugera led the way into the Dufrost area. This area north of Stuartburn and Rosa was in the rich black soil belt. He was followed by others: Manchulenkos, Tkachyks, Kohuts, Derbawka, Pankiw and Kasian. Settling on better lands they made better progress as farmers than their former neighbours . Mr. Pankiw succeeded also as an apiarist and horticulturist.

On the start they did not mix much with the French and even organized a Ukrainian Orthodox parish. Subsequently, there were intermarriages, and further relocations depleted the Ukrainian community at Dufrost. The resettlement at Dufrost showed that on better land Ukrainians enlarged their holdings; some now operate 6,000 acre farms.

There were other examples of farmers who received their start in the original Oleskiw settlement who went west and succeeded. Such was the case of W. Kohut, now of Kelowna, B.C. who acquired a good farm in the Souris area. His son now operates a large farm there and is doing well.

Another example is Matthew Tkachyk. Originally Tkachyks settled on the "border line" south of Tolstoi, and Matthew who worked in the Portage la Prairie plains where he gained experience as a farm machine operator and mechanic now operates a farm of large acreage in the Elm Creek area. This "master farmer" uses equipment of a highly specialized type to meet the demands of cultivating his diversified crops. "And what I can't buy to suit my needs," says Matthew Tkachyk, "I make it myself."

1 Isidore Goresky, Memoirs unpublished, p.140

Conclusion

The establishment of the first Ukrainian settlement in Manitoba in 1896, and news of its initial success served as a magnet to attract thousands to the "promised land", Canada. And the start for this great Ukrainian migration has to be credited to Dr. Joseph Oleskiw. In this first volume about the settlement of Ukrainians east of the Red River, this great leader is given due credit and a hope is expressed that he may receive due recognition by Canadian historians.

Getting established in the area south-east of the Red River was a demanding task, yet undaunted by difficulties the Ukrainian people established a proud record as citizens of their adopted motherland, Canada.

The story is not complete. And it is up to the younger generation to commence making a fuller record of the settlement's success now that ten decades of time have elapsed. A start has been made though. Suffice it to point out Gardenton as a fitting example: Gardenton museum and facilities offer the grandchildren of the stalwart pioneers a place to meet annually; to pay due respect to their forebearers; to renew the pride in their lineage; to rejoice in the progress the younger generation has made as Canadian citizens and with song and dance to mark it as an occasion of joy.

Therefore, in conclusion it is necessary to re-stress the contributions of men like Dr. Joseph Oleskiw, Rev. Iwan Wolanski, Rev. Nestor Dmytriw and tens of leaders who helped to guide the people to a better future. We must give credit to hundreds of men and women who improved their chances in life through better education and through acquiring business skills. They have made a good account of themselves.

Nevertheless, the community as a whole did experience years of stress – the Spanish flu; two world wars and the cursed depression years. However, by maintaining their culture and heritage it became easier for the people to fit into the mold of the good life and wonderful spirit Canadianism provided for all in the Land of Promise. And the Ukrainians merit credit for joining with other Canadians in making Canada a wonderful country.

APPENDISES

Appendix I

OLESKIW, DR. JOSEPH (1860-1903)

Dr. Oleskiw was born in Skvariava Nova, district of Zhovka, Halychyna, the son of a Ukrainian Catholic clergyman. On the completion of his public school education he attended the *Gymnasium* at Lviw, and after eight years of study obtained his baccalaureate in 1878. He studied in the Faculty of Arts at the University of Lviw, majoring in botany, chemistry, and geology. Oleskiw then continued on with post-graduate studies, which culminated in the Ph.D. degree. He married the adopted daughter of Reverend Budzynowskyi and left for Erfurt, Germany, to take up specialized studies in botany, agriculture, and political economy. At Erfurt he wrote several papers on fruit-growing and dairying which were subsequently published. On his return from abroad, Dr. Oleskiw became a lecturer at the Agricultural College at Dublany, near Lviw, and on passing the prescribed examinations, he was appointed Professor of Agriculture of the Teachers' Seminary at Lviw.

Dr. Oleskiw had four children – two daughters and two sons. The eldest daughter, Sophie, born in 1886 (her married name was Fedorchak), later became the principal of the girls' school of the Ukrainian Pedagogical Society at Lviw. She died in 1943. Oleskiw's younger daughter, Maria, became a pianist, and his sons studied engineering.

On the death of his first wife in 1899 Oleskiw remarried. After his appointment as director of the Teachers' Seminary at Sokal, he moved to that town in 1900. Not long afterwards, he became ill and died on October 18, 1903, at the age of forty-three. He was buried in the Ychakiw cemetery at Lviw.

Dr. Oleskiw belonged to the younger generation of his era, which was brought up on Western, progressive ideas, with the stress on democratic principles, as opposed to the conservative tendencies of the older generation. Together with others who believed in these ideas, he set about working for the betterment of the status of the Ukrainian peasantry. Driven to despair by the lack of land – a situation caused mainly by the constant dwindling of landholdings due to partitioning through inheritance – the peasants of Halychyna looked to emigration as their salvation.*

---

* V.J. Kaye, Early Ukrainian Settlements.

**A suburb of Edmonton has recently been named Oleskiw.

Appendix II

Rev. John Wolanski, even after his recall from the USA to western Ukraine, continued to show interest in the emigration of Ukrainians to Canada. Here we include his letter of recommendation to assist Mr. Gregory Czorney to leave for Canada.

(Letter provided by granddaughter, Mrs. Don (Linda) MacKintosh of Coquitlam, B.C.)

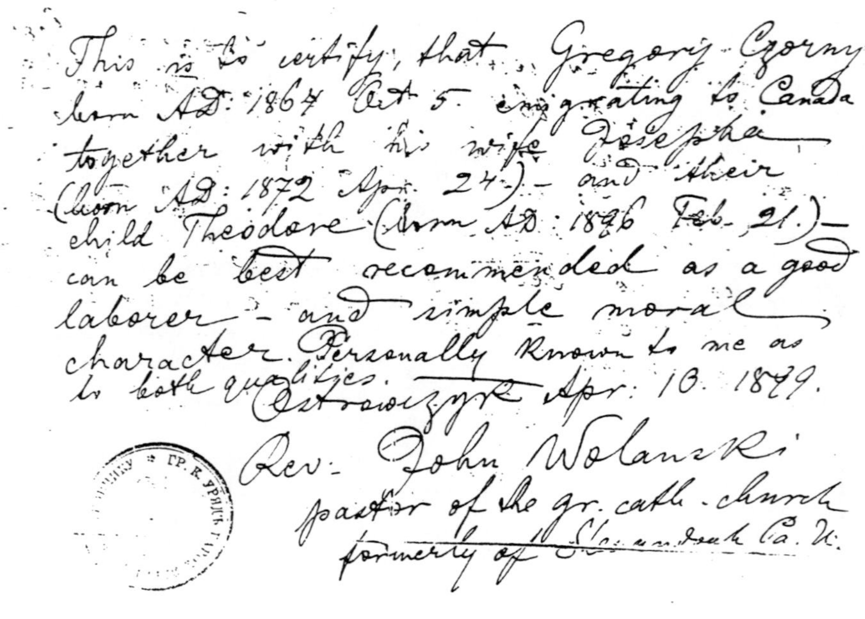
This is to certify, that Gregory Czorny born A.D. 1867 Oct 5. emigrating to Canada together with his wife Josepha (born A.D. 1872 Apr. 24.) – and their child Theodore (born A.D. 1896 Feb. 21.) – can be best recommended as a good laborer – and simple moral character. Personally known to me as to both qualities.

Ostrowczyk Apr. 10. 1899.

Rev. John Wolanski
pastor of the gr. cath. church
formerly of Shenandoah Pa. U.

Appendix III

Kgrylo Genik

It was he that Dr. Oleskiw selected to lead his second group to Canada and the first to Manitoba. A school teacher by training, a man of radical views who got interest in North America through his contacts with Rev. Aghapius Honcharenko in California. An alert man who, no doubt, on Prof. Oleskiw's suggestion and as reported by Michael Stashyn in his memoirs studied English with the aid of a German English dictionary while crossing the Atlantic.

On settling in Stuartburn where he selected a homestead he was available to provide his group with advice. In this first Manitoba group there were several of his countrymen from Beriziw.

However, having mastered the rudiments of English and knowing German, the Canadian immigration officials moved him to Winnipeg to act as interpreter. It was, therefore, in this sphere of the settlement of the west by Ukrainians that he made the greatest positive contribution and in time as a C.P.R. employment agent who made several trips to the Ukraine to recruit labourers for the construction of railway lines in Canada.

Regrettably, however, his name is not recorded with other men who contributed to the development of the west by building networks of railway lines and neither have the Ukrainian labourers received due credit. In time they not only provided service as ordinary section hands but as section foreman. It is regrettable that thus far there has not been an in-depth research in the records of the Canadian Railway lines about the contribution of Ukrainians in the field of Canadian transportation.

Mr. Genik kept in touch with the Ukrainian poet Iwan Franko, Rev. Aghapius Honcharenko in California and other progressive radicals in Kolomyja. Regrettably his records and correspondence were destroyed in one of Winnipeg's floods.

Appendix IV

Rev. Nestor Dmytriw

The fourth man to appear on the scene to provide guidance to the Oleskiw settlers bound for the Canadian North West Territories was Rev. Nestor Dmytriw. In a letter of Lord Strathcona to Clifford Sifton we read:

> Father Dmytriw has now been engaged permanently to look after these people and we will have less difficulty in settling them then heretofore...and show them that it is to their own interest to follow the suggestions of the Government in the matter of location.*

Rev. Dmytriw first came to the west as a missionary. He first visited the Ukrainian settlers in the Edmonton region. And as a missionary he was successful. Then he visited the Drifting River settlement; and like a true missionary he walked from Valley River the seven miles to the Ksionzek home. Here the first child to be baptized was named Petrunella. The settlement became known as the Terembola settlement. He left a permanent historical record of his visit.

At Trembola when the settlers assembled from the homesteads around, it is claimed that he was taken across Drifting River seated on a black ox. He sang mass in the house and across the river consecrated the Cross of Freedom. There have been pilgrimages to the Cross of Freedom annually. It is now an historical site. The Cross of Freedom is an indication of how Ukrainians accepted their adopted homeland and treasure that freedom to this day.

In his short sermon at the Cross of Freedom, he exhorted the settlers to cherish the promise the new land provided.

Credit is due to both Rev. Wolanski and Rev. Dmytriw for their progressive approaches and their mastering of the English language. As an immigration officer he tried to get the Ukrainian settlers to come to Canada. I his letter of 27 January 1898, he warned the Canadian Government that steamship company agents were recruiting Ukrainian settlers to Argentina (some 10,000 in number) and that the services of Dr. Oleskiw were required to divert these people to Canada.

* Oles/60332 July 15, 1898. Lord Strathcona to Clifford Sifton, July 11, 1898.

Bibliography

Anniversary Year Book Ukrainian National Home, Vita, MB, June 1979.

Balan, Jars. Salt and Braided Bread: Ukrainian Life in Canada, Oxford University Press, Toronto, 1984.

Berton, Pierre. The Promised Land: Settling the West 1896-1914, A Penguin Books Canada, McLelland and Stewart Book, 1990.

Coates, Ken and McGuinness, Fred. Manitoba: The Province and The People, Hurtig Press, Edmonton 1987.

Dmytriw, Nestor. Canadian Ruthenia, Memoirs, M. H. Marunchak, editor, UVAN Winnipeg, 1972.

Ewanchuk, Michael. Vita: A Ukrainian Community, Bk I, II and III. Derksen Printers, Steinbach, MB, 1977.

Ewanchuk, Michael. Pioneer Profiles: Ukrainian Settlers in Manitoba, Derksen Printers, Steinbach, MB, 1981.

Gerus, O. W. and Rea, J. E. The Ukrainians in Canada, Canadian Historical Society, Ottawa, ON, 1988.

Humeniuk, Peter. Hardships and Progress of Ukrainian Pioneers (Memoirs), Steinbach, MB, 1977.

Lupul, Manoly R. A Heritage in Transition: Essays in the History of Ukrainians in Canada, McLelland and Stewart, Toronto, 1982.

Marunchak, M. H. The Ukrainian Canadians: A History, UVAN Winnipeg, 1982.

Murchie, R. W. and H. C. Grant. Unused Lands of Manitoba, Manitoba Department of Agriculture, 1926.

Myshuha, Luke. Jubilee Book of Ukrainian National Association, 40th Anniversary Jersey City, N.Y., USA, 1936.

Panchuk, John. Bukovinian Settlements in Southern Manitoba (Gardenton, MB) Baute Creek, Mich., April 1971.

Oleskiw, Joseph. About Free Lands, Republished with Introduction by M. H. Marunchak, Winnipeg, 1975.

Paximadis, Mary. Look Who's Coming; The Wachna Story, Miracle Press Ltd., Oshawa, 1976.

Pinuta, Harry. Land of Pain Land of Promise, Western Producer Prairie Books, Saskatoon, 1978.

Yuzyk, Paul. The Ukrainians in Manitoba: A Social History, University of Toronto Press, 1953.

Index

Other books by the same author:

Pioneer Settlers: Ukrainians in the Dauphin Area 1896-1926.
Vita: A Ukrainian Community (a set of three books).
Spruce, Swamp and Stone: A History of the Pioneer Ukrainian Settlements in the Gimli Area.
Pioneer Profiles: Ukrainian Settlers in Manitoba.
Hawaiian Ordeal: Ukrainian Contract Workers 1897-1910.
Young Cossack, a novella,
Reflections and Reminiscences: Ukrainians in Canada 1892-1992.
William Kurelek: The Suffering Genius
Pioneer Settlements: Ukrainians in Canada (in Ukrainian)